ANTONIO SOMERA

In His Own Words

Jose M. Fraguas

EMPIRE BOOKS/AWP LLC
Los Angeles, California

INGRAM
Disclaimer
Please note that the author and publisher of this book are NOT RESPONSIBLE in any manner whatsoever for any injury that may result from practicing the techniques and/or following the instructions given within. Since the physical activities described herein may be too strenuous in nature for some readers to engage in safely, it is essential that a physician be consulted prior to training.

First Edition published in 2022 by AWP LLC/Empire Books.
Copyright (c) 2022 by AWP LLC/Empire Books.

All rights reserved. No part of this publication may be reproduced or utilized in any form or by any means, electronic or mechanical, including photo- copying, recording, or by any information storage and retrieval system, without prior written permission from AWP LLC/Empire Books.

Library of Congress Catalog ISBN-13: 978-1-949753-52-3

22 21 20 19 18 17 16 15 14 13 12 11 10

Library of Congress Cataloging-in-Publication Data

In His Own Words Antonio Somera by Jose M. Fraguas – Compiled & Arranged ed. p. cm.

ISBN 978-1-949753-52-3 (pbk. : alk. paper)
1. Martial arts– philosophy. 3. Large type books. I. Title.
 GV1114.3.F224 20143261.815'4–dc22

20060108673

Printed in the United States of America.

"Practitioners should focus on the general benefits of martial arts, from self-defense to using it as a way to achieve a better life, instead of trying to be a deadly fighting machine. We should strive to be better human beings – that should be the final goal of any martial art. Our goal should be to avoid fighting and to preserve life, not take enjoyment in hurting others and destroying life."

- *Grandmaster Emeritus Leo M. Giron*

Dedication

I dedicate this book to the memory of Antonio Somera.

Acknowledgments

Many people were responsible for making this book possible, some more directly than others. I want to extend my gratitude to all those whom so generously contributed their time and experience to the preparation of this work.

To Masters Kirk McCune and Joel Juanitas for his assistance during the photographic session.

To all the "Bahalana Escrima" instructors who shared and still teach their knowledge and experience with students around the world.

The "Giron Escrima" legacy lives on thanks to you.

You all have my enduring thanks.

— Jose M. Fraguas

About the Author

Born and raised in Madrid, Spain, Jose M. Fraguas began his martial arts studies with judo, in grade school, at age 9. From there he moved to study to other arts. In 1980, he moved to Los Angeles, California, where his open-minded mentality helped him to develop a more elaborated approach to the martial arts. His training in Filipino Martial Arts started that year at the old "Kali Academy" owned by Guro Dan Inosanto in Torrance, California. His Escrima journey and tutelage under Guro Inosanto led him to train with other legendary masters from whom he learned different Kali and Arnis approaches and methods to the Filipino Martial Arts. He began his career as a writer at age 16 as a regular contributor to martial arts magazines in Great Britain, France, Spain, Italy, Germany, Portugal, Holland and Australia. In 1980, he moved to Los Angeles, California, where his open-minded mentality helped him to develop a more elaborated approach to the martial arts.

Fraguas founded his first publishing company in Europe, authoring dozens of books and distributing his magazines to 35 countries in three different languages. His reputation and credibility as a martial artist and publisher became well known to the top masters around the world. Considering himself a martial artist first and a writer and publisher second, Fraguas feels fortunate to have had the opportunity to interview many legendary martial artists. He recognizes that much of the information given in the interviews helped him to discover new dimensions in the martial arts. "I was constantly absorbing knowledge from the great masters," he recalls. "I only trained with a few of them, but intellectually, academically and spiritually all of them have made very important contributions to my growth as a complete martial artist."

Steeped in tradition yet looking to the future, Fraguas understands and appreciates martial arts history and philosophy and feels this rich heritage is a necessary steppingstone to personal growth and spiritual evolution. His desire to promote both ancient philosophy and modern thinking provided the motivation for writing this book. "If the motivation is just money, a book cannot be of good quality,"

Fraguas says. "If the book is written to just make people happy, it cannot be deep. I want to write books so I can learn as well as teach. Martial Arts, like human life itself, are filled with experiences that seem quite ordinary at the time and assume a fabled stature only with the passage of the years. I hope this work will be appreciated by future practitioners not only of the Filipino Martial Arts but for all martial arts in general, regardless of the style."

It is clear that every one of us will some kind of leave a legacy behind when we die. The challenge is the same for all of us. For Fraguas, who has authored more than 30 books, the important question is what kind of legacy will I leave? "I believe our main legacy as writers is to educate or even just re-echo those things that we believe are worthwhile - a subjective matter. Even if the idea is obvious or simple, we believe it deserves to be kept alive, and we do that using different ways current with the times; we broadcast our worldview with our family, friends, co-workers, and so on," he says. "Ideally we live by our beliefs so as to lend them credence; the "unfollowing adherent" is just a meaningless mouthpiece - a preacher not following his own sermon. A legacy of values proven out by the bearer's own life would be a very good legacy for anyone. Life is motion, and the real goal of a writer should be to arrest that motion [which is life] and preserve knowledge [the words of this master in this book] by artificial means, and hold it fixed so that a hundred years later, when a stranger opens a book and reads it, it moves again since it is life. Since man is mortal, the only immortality possible for a writer is to leave something behind him that is immortal since it will always move. This is the writer's way of scribbling "I was here" on the wall of the final and irrevocable oblivion through which we all must someday pass."

Jose M. Fraguas lives in Los Angeles, California.

TABLE OF CONTENTS

INTRODUCTION .... **X**

INTERVIEW **1**

WRITINGS **28**

   COMING TO AMERICA **30**

   GROWING UP IN AMERICA **32**

   DREAMS COME TRUE **34**

   PLAYING THE ART IN SECRET **36**

   WHAT HAS BEEN LEARNED **38**

   ESCRIMA LODGE **40**

   THE HIDDEN TREASURE **42**

   SITUATIONS CHANGE **48**

   HOMECOMING FOR DAN INOSANTO .. **52**

   BANDA-BANDA **58**

   LARGO MANO: THE WARRIOR STYLE **60**

ESCRIMA TECHNIQUES 64

- SINGLE LAPEL GRAB 66
- SINGLE LAPEL GRAB OPPOSITE VIEW . 68
- DOUBLE LAPEL GRAB 70
- DOUBLE NECK GRAB 71
- REVERSE WRIST GRAB 72
- WRIST GRAB FROM THE BACK 73
- BEAR HUG FROM THE BACK 74
- DEFENSE AGAINST TACKLE................. 75
- FRONTAL LAPEL GRAB ON A CHAIR 76
- SHOULDER GRAB FROM THE SIDE 77
- POINTING GUN FROM THE BACK 78
- KNIFE ATTACK FROM THE FRONT 80
- BLADE DEFENSE AGAINST ANGLE #2 .. 82
- STICK DEFENSE AGAINST ANGLE #2 ... 83
- DEFENSE AGAINST ANGLE #5 84

Introduction

Grandmaster Antonio "Tony" Somera was a lifelong resident of Stockton, California.

Few are the chosen ones fortunate enough to be close to legendary names of the martial arts world. Even fewer individuals have the privilege of sharing their lives with great masters, in-and-out of the training hall, learning from their experiences, and listening everyday to a wealth of wisdom and knowledge only gathered by a handful of martial arts instructors. Master Tony Somera was one of the few. He spent many years of his life with the late grandmaster Leo Giron. Grandmaster Giron selected Somera to become the heir of his system, and the relationship both men shared until the day Giron passed away was unique. Their bonding was beyond martial arts — their relationship was like a father and son.

Sponsored by his father, Celestino Somera and Leo Giron, he became a member in good standing of the "Legionarios Del Trabajo General Luna" lodge in 1980. GM Somera was a life member of the lodge and was transferred to become a member of the "Daguhoy" lodge.

One of the reasons for the transfer was because of his work on a "Filipino American Museum" that he created at the Daguhoy Lodge building. GM Somera discovered the vast treasures now held in the museum collection while doing some cleaning at the lodge during the transition of the "Bahala Na Martial Arts Association" from their training club located in North Stockton to South Stockton. Over the years many people had lived at the lodge. Stored in the basement, and almost forgotten, were years of personal mementos left behind as the fortunes of life fluctuated. There were pictures, posters, newspapers, magazines, personal and group photos, musical scores, poetry, essays, letters and even books of jokes that were written by the "manongs" (elders). There were beds, tables and chairs from the period. There were receipts and ledgers from small businesses of the time. There were zoot suits, clothes, watches, lighters and other personal items. GM Somera even found a hand forged sword, spear and shield. Some of the most striking items are the many military medals, memorabilia and uniforms that were left behind as the heroic Filipino American soldiers, who fought for our country in WWII, moved on to continue their normal lives. These World War II veterans were from the world famous and highly decorated 1st and 2nd Filipino Infantry along with General Douglas MacArthur's 978th Signal Crop. They were the first known commandos of their caliber during World War II history.

Along with members of the Bahala Na® Martial Arts, GM Somera renovated the space and put the collected materials in order for viewing. They created a museum space that approximates the living conditions of the time being displayed along with unique and fascinating objects that make history come alive. It is a wonderful snap shot back in time of a dynamic period in Stockton history and American history!

He was a life member of FALNHS and on the board of trustees for the "Little Manila Foundation" since 2002. The "Filipino American National Historical Society" (FANHS) is truly a community-based organization whose mission is "...to preserve, document, and present Filipino American history and to support scholarly research and artistic works which reflect that rich past...". The "Little Manila Foundation" advocates for the historic preservation of the "Little Manila Historic Site" in Stockton, California and provides education and leadership to revitalize the Filipino/American community.

Along with the community service, GM Somera was also a leader in the martial arts community. He was a 3rd degree black belt in Goju Ryu Karate gained in 1974. He was also the highest ranking student and vice president in Mande Muda Silat.

However, he was most well known for being Grand Master Tony Somera of the "Bahala Na® Martial Arts", "Giron® Arnis Escrima". As a direct result of superior skill and devotion to the principles, philosophy and purpose of "Bahala Na Martial Arts" combined with leadership and his master level Instructorship, Master Tony Somera was promoted to the rank and responsibility of Grand Master by the late Grand Master and founder of "Bahala Na® Martial Arts" Leo M. Giron. Grand Master Somera promoted the art of "Giron® Arnis Escrima" along with its rich Filipino History and culture by providing opportunities for students and community members to visit historic sites and learn Filipino American history through bi-annual "affiliate camps" held in Stockton. GM Tony Somera was the only person ever to be promoted to the rank of Master and then Grand Master by the late Grand Master Emeritus Leo M. Giron.

By Jose M. Fraguas

ONE ON ONE

WITH

ANTONIO SOMERA

1

TONY SOMERA: In His Own Words

Q: How long have you been practicing the martial arts?

A: I began when I was nine. We just have to do the math.

Q: How many styles of escrima or other methods have you trained in?

A: In 1976, I started my escrima training with Gilbert Tino, a master in the decuerdas system. But that would only last for about six months. After questioning my father about Filipino martial arts, my father finally directed me to go and see my Uncle Leo (Leo Giron). My father had referred to Leo Giron as my uncle because my father and Giron belonged to the same Filipino fraternal order and one of the strongest Filipino lodges ... the Legionarios Del Trabajo in America.

I remember that a friend and karate student of mine was also researching Filipino arts. One day we decided to go to visit Uncle Leo. I remember the first day of training with him. We got out of our car and walked toward Uncle Leo's house. There he was watering his front lawn before class had begun. Uncle Leo looked up at me and said, "You have grown since last time I have seen you. How are your mom and dad?" As we went to the backyard, all I could remember is that he was trying to catch up on my life and what I have been doing. He also talked about farming and how my mom and dad were very hard workers. That whole evening during class as I watched other young students "play" (as Uncle Leo would referred training too). I was jumping at the correct time to ask permission to "play" with him. I felt like he was interviewing me for a job. Finally, almost at the end of class, he asked me if I would like to play. By that time, the class was just about over, and he said to come back to the next class on Wednesday. I returned that next Wednesday and started my formal training in Giron arnis escrima.

Q: Tell us some interesting stories of your early days in martial arts training with grandmaster Leo Giron.

A ONE ON ONE INTERVIEW

A: One time grandmaster Giron and I went to visit a local martial art supply store in Stockton, California. At the time there was an escrima class going on in the back room, and Giron wanted to visit the teacher. In the meantime, we were looking at the different martial art supplies. Of course, the rattan sticks caught the grandmaster's eye. The sales person said, "I noticed you are looking at the escrima sticks." The grandmaster replied, "Yes, is that what you call them?" The sales person said that these were special combat fighting weapons that are used for a style called larga mano. Well, the grandmaster perked up and said, "Larga Mano?" The sales person said yes, adding that this is the style of Leo Giron and that he was his teacher. The grandmaster looked at me with a smile and said, "Who is this Leo Giron?" The sales person said he is the father of larga mano in America and then he went on to explain the larga mano system. It was like watching the fox in a hen house. Eventually, the guro from the school came out to greet grandmaster Giron. When he walked out, he turned to the sales person and said, "This is grandmaster Leo Giron." I think the sales person was a little embarrassed. We all had a big laugh and after enjoyed causal conversation.

Q: How was your personal relationship with Gradmaster Leo Giron?

A: He was like a father to me. And I know he thought of me like if I was his family. We were very close, closer than many family members are. There was an special bond between us. It was like if that relationship between us was meant to be the way it was.

Q: With all the technical changes during the last decades, do you think there are still pure styles of escrima or kali?

A: I can only speak of our system of escrima because I have not trained enough in the art of kali. So, having said that, I feel strongly that our system of escrima is still pure. The only things that have changed have been the different applications against the different types of weapons and aggressive opponents. As a second-generation escrimador, I have the opportunity to apply the different playing techniques in many different and exciting ways. The basic fundamentals are the same and should never change.

Q: How do you see Filipino martial arts in America at the present time?

A: I feel that this is a great time in history for Filipino martial arts in America. The Filipino arts are growing. As more Americans explore the arts, they will experience and see the effectiveness the Filipino martial arts have to offer. Not only in the physi-

TONY SOMERA: In His Own Words

cal application of defensive protection but also in the rich Filipino culture and history. In the first half of the 1900s, Filipinos were the backbone of agriculture development in America. In the early 1900s, California — and in particular Stockton — had the greatest population of Filipino's. As a result, Stockton received the name "Little Manila."

Q: Does it enhance the empty hand aspect of the art to train with weapons?

A: Yes, but you need to understand — as a teacher or student — the role the weapon will play in a confrontation, along

with the role that empty hands will have as the extension of the weapon. In the Giron system, we start training the student first with the weapon and then apply the same knowledge to the empty-hand application. I have found that the weapon training has enhanced the empty hand application and in most cases will increase your hand speed and accuracy.

Q: You are the only practitioner of the Giron arnis escrima system ever to be awarded the title of master. And now, more recently, you were appointed by Leovigildo M. Giron, the system's founder, as the new Grandmaster of the art. Can you tell us how this came about and how this makes you feel?

A: Yes, it is true that I was awarded the rank of master by then grandmaster Leo M. Giron on Oct. 3, 1992. At the time grandmaster Giron was looking at the future of his Giron arnis escrima system and the Bahala Na Martial Arts Association to assure that his art will continue to exist and that his work would live on and grow. This was such a tremendous honor for me and at the time was so unbelievable, only because the title of master was always reserved for the manongs (elder Filipinos) or legends of the arts.

On Dec. 1, 1999 I was appointed by grandmaster Leo M. Giron to the rank of grandmaster. Given manong Leo's health, his intent to promote me from master to grandmaster would provide the organization with little or no transition upon his

A ONE ON ONE INTERVIEW

passing and will endure that the growth and direction of the organization will continue as he has directed it during his tenure.

Again with grandmaster Giron's ability to structure the art and the organization he had founded, his master plan is to have his art continue so the art would live on through all of us forever. This appointment from master to grandmaster was truly an indescribable honor for me. It is an honor to know that grandmaster Giron has the confidence in me to continue his work in the responsibility to maintain the highest quality of art as propagated. Grandmaster Giron continues to serve in an advisory capacity as grandmaster emeritus.

Q: Mamy people came to know of Leo Giron and his Largo Mano (long range) system in the 1970s as a result of publicity given to him by guro Dan Inosanto. Can you tell us how Mr. Inosanto first came to meet and study under manong Leo?

A: I will relay this story as it was told to me by grandmaster Giron: Dan Inosanto's mother and father were very good friends with Leo Giron and his wife, Alberta. They all belonged to the same church, they would attend social events together and when the Girons moved to Stockton in the early 1970s they only lived one block away from the Inosanto family. In September, 1968, Leo Giron had already established a licensed escrima club in Tracy, Calif., but because of their move to Stockton, Giron relocated his club to the basement and backyard of his home in Stockton. At this time Dan was looking throughout the United States for the old veterans and teachers of escrima. In fact, Dan had already found and met many escrimadors from Stockton and Hawaii.

During a wedding of a daughter of a local Filipino family, Mary Inosanto, Dan's mother approached Leo Giron to inquirer about Giron's teaching of escrima. Giron, being a quiet and humble man, listened to Mary Inosanto about how Daniel was looking for

TONY SOMERA: In His Own Words

someone to teach him "the real escrima," meaning the combative style or estilo matador.

Giron's first reply was that he knew of no one. Mary would not take no for an answer and further replied, "Leo, because of your service in the military during World War II and the jungle warfare you had to endure, I know you must have the real escrima." Mary was very persistent and finally Giron gave in and said, "I think I may know of someone who can help you." Giron was thinking of someone else at the time, another escrimador from Sta. Catalina Ilocos Sur, Philippines named Joe Pacpaco, who was a member of the Mabini Lodge in Stockton. Giron and Pacpaco would train occasionally in Giron's basement and at the lodge. That night after the wedding Mary Inosanto called Dan to inform him of her discovery. That same night Dan called manong Leo and informed him that he would be driving up the next day to talk and hopefully train with Giron. Well the next day Dan showed up with a magazine writer and photographer. They talked and Giron preformed a few techniques with Dan. Dan had found what he was looking for. After that meeting, Dan and manong Leo became very close friends and as Dan has said many times manong Leo is like a second father to him.

Following their meeting in the summer of 1970 Dan would travel to Stockton many times, and during vacation the Girons would go to Los Angles to visit family. During their visits Dan, along with Richard Bustillo, Ted Lucay Lucay, and Jerry Poteet, would pick manong Leo up and bring him to their academy in Carson to train. Several years later in December of 1973 Dan would be the first student to graduate from the Giron system. To this day Dan and manong Leo remain very close and still communicate.

A ONE ON ONE INTERVIEW

TONY SOMERA: In His Own Words

Q: Despite the fact that Mr. Inosanto and others came to learn and help promote Giron's largo mano style, this is but one small piece of the entire Giron arnis escrima system. For those who are unfamiliar with the system in total, would you offer a brief overview of its various subsystems and components?

A: Grandmaster Giron is well-known around the world for his larga mano style of escrima. But, as you say, this is just a small piece of the entire Giron arnis escrima system. The Giron system has 20 styles and techniques that are just as effective and just as complete. Here are the names and a brief overview of each of the 20 styles (estilo) that encompass the Giron arnis escrima system.

1. **Estilo de Fondo** — This is a style of planting yourself firmly on the ground. During combat you do not want to move your feet about, as this may cause you to lose your footing and balance. This style counters off the 12 angles of attack using a stick in length of 24 inches which simulates the bolo. There are approximately 160 countermovements in this style.

2. **Estilo de Abanico** — This is a fanning style encompassing the use of the side of the weapon (stick or blade) to block oncoming attacks. Counterstriking is included with the emphasis on the tip of your weapon to get the maximum amount of power in short and powerful striking ranges.

3. **Estilo Abierta** — This style refers to an open body style of fighting. This style is used by the most advanced students to calculate the distance between themselves and their opponent. The student will calculate the opponent's strikes and will open his body position and counterstrike within the same motion, leaving the opponent with little or no counter.

A ONE ON ONE INTERVIEW

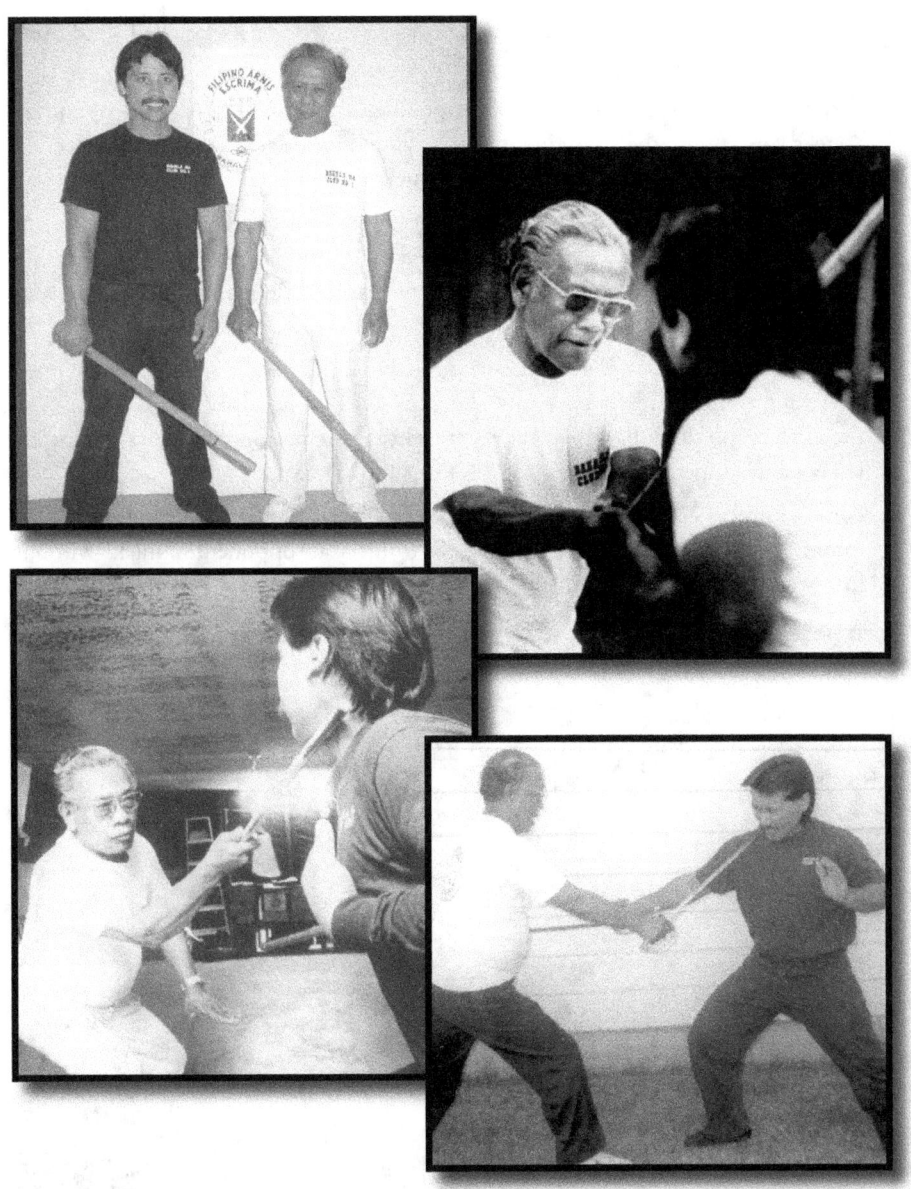

"Escrima teaches you how to deal with attacks based on the angle they are delivered...and not in the specifics of the tool used for the attack."

TONY SOMERA: In His Own Words

4. **Estilo de Salon** — This is a dance-like style. This style uses fast and solid footwork that also involves the use of stickwork.

5. **Estilo Sonkete** — This is the style of poking and thrusting. As your opponent attacks you can use the components of parrying, blocking, evading, and deflection while applying the counterthrust or poke into the opponent's guard.

6. **Estilo Retirada** — This is a style of retreating used to draw your opponent in or to create an opening in the opponent's defense. Once this has taken place you can use counterstriking to render your opponent helpless. Retreating footwork, evading, and counterstriking is the key.

7. **Estilo Elasico** — An elastic-like or rubber band style. It makes use of one's stretching ability to reach a given target. This style is a necessity that is woven into the larga mano (long hand) style. Many feel that the person who plays estilo elasico possesses superhuman ability and is difficult to defeat.

8. **Fondo Fuerte** — The escrimador's last stand. You must plant yourself effectively into a reliable spot where you can revolve to meet an opponent's attacks without losing ground.

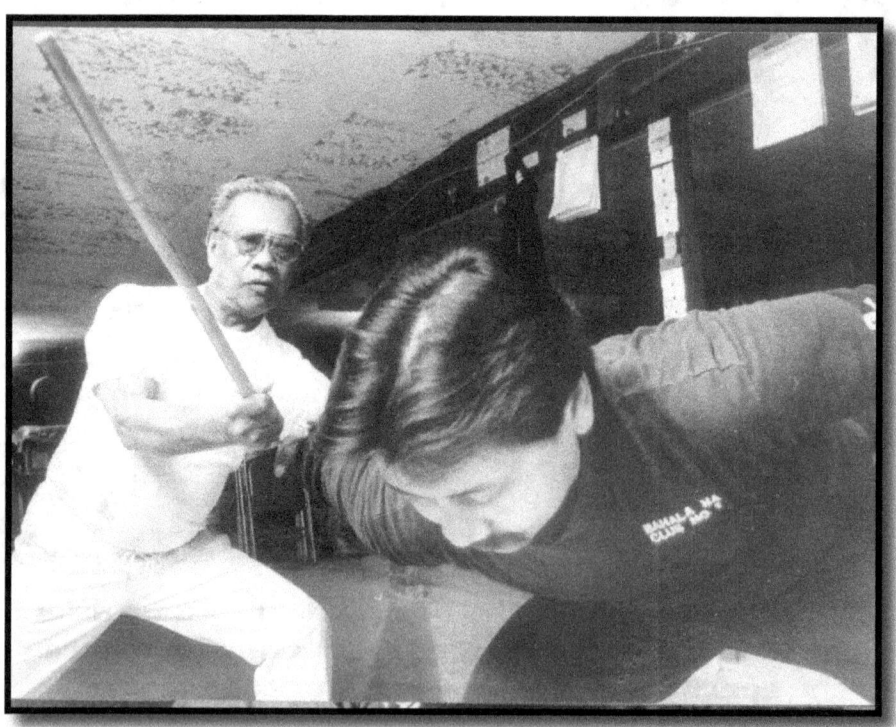

A ONE ON ONE INTERVIEW

9. **Contra Compas** — These Spanish words mean against time. In terms of Giron arnis escrima this is a style of striking with off-beat timing or broken rhythm.

10. **Estlio Redonda** — This is a round or circular style of fighting. To be effective in this style you must be able to maneuver your strikes in circular movements horizontally, vertically, and diagonally, from both high and low positions.

11. **Combate Adentro** — This style is used to ward off opponents using paired weapons, such as the sword and dagger. With this style, you defend yourself inside the opponent's circle using solid footwork and slicing counterstrikes.

12. **Tero Grave** — This style implies the use of serious or deadly strikes to critical areas of the body.

13. **Estilo Macabebe** — Macabebe is the name of a town in the province of Pampanga, Philippines. These fierce warriors are famous for the use of two weapons or two sticks. This style is characterized by the interweaving motions of the weapons and is also known as sinawali.

14. **Tero Pisada** — This style incorporates the use of double or two-handed striking and blocking. The blocking is so intense that it will paralyze the opponent's hands and will create an opening for your two-handed counterstrike.

TONY SOMERA: In His Own Words

15. **Media Media** — The term media media implies half of half. In terms of fighting, the concept refers to fighting at half-range and striking on half-timing.

16. **Cadena de Mano** — This is a hand-to-hand combat method which uses parrying, grabbing, twisting, locking, and chocking in succession. In other words, you chain the hand movements together from close quarters.

17. **Escapo** — This style stresses evasion and methods of warding off the opponents

18. **Estilo Bolante** — This style is named after a person named Braulio Bolante from Dagupan, Pagasinan, Philippines. This style uses vertical striking patterns and is an excellent method of fighting in doorways and narrow passages.

19. **Miscla Contras** — This style favors defending yourself against multiple opponents and multiple attacks. It stresses placing oneself in the proper place and position in relation to the opponent.

20. **Largo mano** — This style maintains long-distance fighting without jeopardizing safety. The counter concept is that of attacking the closest target of your opponent and to terminate the contest with the first counterstrike.

Q: It appears that the Giron system is well-rounded and complete in terms of conceptual fighting methods. Can you give us some background on the systems that Giron learned and their masters?

A: Manong Leo had five teachers and I will give them to you in order and what style they played.

1. Benito Junio from the barrio of Inerangan town of Bayombang province of Pangasinan, Luzon Philippines. In 1920 young Giron started his education in arnis escrima. Benito Junio was famous for his larga mano (long hand-stick) and fondo fuerte (fighting in a solid position) styles.

A ONE ON ONE INTERVIEW

2. Fructuso Junio from the barrio of Telbang town of Bayombang provice of Pangasinan, Luzon Philippines. From 1921-1926 Giron continued his training with Fructuso uncle to Bentio. Fructuso Junio was well-known for his Macabebe or two-stick fighting. Fructuso was the first to share with Giron the importance of distinguishing between the old (cada-anan) and new (cabaroan) styles of Luzon.

3. Flavian Vergara from Santa Curz in Llocos Sur Luzon, Philippines. Vergara was the top student of Dalmacio Bergonia who defeated the great champion Santiago Toledo. Vergara and Giron started their training in the prune orchards of Meridian, Calif., from 1929-1932. Vergara and Giron would meet again directly after the outbreak of World War II. Their lives would cross for the last time in October 1942 when Giron was shipped out to Fort Ord, Calif. Every spare minute Vergara and Giron would train until Giron was shipped out in January, 1943. Vergara was a master in the Bergonia style and very proficient in the estilo elastico (rubber band style). Giron had said that Vergara had superhuman abilities. Vergara influenced Giron and his understanding of the relationships between the cada-anan (old) and cabaroan (new) styles of arnis escrima.

4. Beningo Ramos from Kongkong Bayongbang. During World War II Ramos was a sergeant in the Filipino army assigned to Sergeant Giron. Pryor to the outbreak of World War II Ramos was an improbable arnis escrima teacher and was respected as one of the best estilo matador (killer-style) teachers in Luzon. Ramos was an expert in larga mano, miscla contras, tero pisada, tero grave and elastico styles. Ramos was so confident of his skills that he and Giron would play with live bolos. Ramos bet Giron that if he could hit him he would give Giron one month's pay. Manong Leo told me he never collected a cent from Ramos.

5. Julian Bundoc from the barrio of Carangay town of Bayombang provice of Pangasianan, Luzon Philippines. Julian was cousin to Benito Junio. Julian Bundoc and Giron would play more of the combative larga mano and work on conditioning the body. Julian Bundoc was also a master of hilot or massage. Giron and Bundoc trained in Stockton from 1956-1961.

One of manong Leo's teachers named Flaviano Vergara had the most influence on young Giron and helped him develop his system called Giron Arnis Escrima.

Q: Of the 20 styles, isn't the first, estilo de fondo, a creation of Leo Giron, as opposed to a system he learned from a teacher?

A: Yes, estilo de fondo is the creation of Leo M. Giron, hence the meaning of patakaran ni gng (Giron). This is the style that Giron was able to use and incorporate

TONY SOMERA: In His Own Words

with the larga mano style he had used during World War II. On the other hand, the main style of Vergara was the Bergonia style that utilized the use of two-handed blocking and counterstriking with either left or right hand. Giron was determined to build a good solid foundation of teaching using the curriculum of the 12 angles of attack with counterblocking and the use of a 24-inch stick to simulate the average-sized bolo knife.

Q: The Giron system of Escrima has many driiling exercises. How important are these in order to effectively fight?

A: Fighting effectively is a very specififc issue. It is not based on a large amount of techniques but in courage, determination and what we can call "killer instinct' or "survival mechanism". The last one, either you have or you don't, regardles of all the academical and technical knowledge you may have.

Combat or fighting is about action and reaction. It is through drilling realistically that you develop these abilities necessary to "react" in combat. It is not necessary spar all the time. Sparring is like "jumping in the deep end of the pool" but in order to learn how to swim you do not need swim in the depth of the ocean.

In order to be safe, you can drill realistically, please note that I say "realistically" – the most of the time, and once in a while wear some protective gear and go into all-out sparring to see how you deal with the pressure of full-contact sparring.

Q: Is Escrima mainly an art of stickfighting?

A: Escrima is not a stickfighting art, it is a blade art. The basics and fundamental principles and techniques of the art are blade oriented. The use of the stick is a training tool but it is noy an stick art. It is true that many maneouvers and techniques are interrelated to the use of the stick but we have to keep in mind that we are practising and training an art based on the use of a bladed weapon.

There are many little details that make a big difference when you have a "stick" mentality or a "blade" mentality. The use and the angle of the body, the positioning

A ONE ON ONE INTERVIEW

of the wrist, the "contras' after an attack, etc, are veru diffeent if we keep the "blade' mentality and do not fall into the trap of thinking that the art is just "stickfighting". Of course there are other components like the empty hand methods, but those are different.

Because the art was developed in war times, the blade training is the first phase, the other elements come after in the training progression.

Q: How much the individual should adapt to the style and how much the style should me modfied to suit the individual?

A: That is a difficult question to answer precisely. A beginner should follow the guidelines of the technical elements of the style withiut "adding" his own flavor to things. Atick to the fundamentals; follow the principles and structure of the style and stick to the methodology taught by the intructor. At that level, the student's understanding is not high enough to add or substract anything.

Fter years of training, study and reaching a high technical level of the system, the student may apply the same principles but in a way that suit them betterto him or her due to certain specifics. At that level, the Esrimador do not change the principles of the art but "plays" with them and express them in a personal way. It is at that level when you can see two exponents of the art using the same principles but physically looking different when they perform. Water is water either it is in an ice cube, being

TONY SOMERA: In His Own Words

A ONE ON ONE INTERVIEW

poured in a glass in a fluid form or in the air in the form of steam. Same element, different expression.

Q Many have written that the late grandmaster Angel Cabales is the Father of Escrima in the United States, because he opened the first commercial school here. What many do not know, however, is that grandmaster Giron was also involved in that school, as was Max Sarmiento and Dentoy Revillar. And yet, in the end they went their own ways. Can you tell us about the events and what transpired at that time?

A: I don't know what, if anything, happened between Max Sarmiento and Dentoy Revillar, but I will give you the information that grandmaster Giron gave me.

Max Sarmiento and his wife, along with Dentoy Revillar, were the three that helped grandmaster Cabales open his first commercial school in Stockton. At the time Giron was training with Dentoy Revillar and Max Sarmiento at Tracy Defense Depot in Tracy, Calif. They would train in the back of a warehouse and between stacks of pallets so no one would see what they were doing. I was told during this training they would train between the pallets and at times Giron would jump from the stacks of pallets to other stacks of pallets to simulate different terrain fighting. They would use anything they could find — from aluminum pipes to broom handles and wide boards as shields.

Dentoy Revillar told me that one time he and Giron were sparring. Revillar thought he had Giron in his angle to catch him with a number-three strike to Giron's left hip. Revillar counterblocked and quickly delivered the number-three strike. Giron, using estilo eslastico, ducked completely under Revillar's strike. Revillar could not believe it.

Meanwhile, Giron had already had the acquaintance of Cabales because of the many social events that were held by the different Filipino lodges in Stockton. One day Cabales, Revillar and Sarmiento invited Giron to come and visit at the Serrada academy located next to Gong Lee's restaurant. Giron, on occasion, would drop in and play and help teach the students that were enrolled at the academy. It was the idea of all to form the biggest arnis escrima academy in the United States. Cabales would teach serrada, Giron would teach larga mano, Sarmiento would teach cadena de mano and Revillar would assist all three. But, in 1968 after the killing of eight student nurses, most of them Filipinas, Giron decided to open his own club in Tracy. But Giron still wanted to associate with Cabales and the rest of the academy.

TONY SOMERA: In His Own Words

One day Giron went to Cabales to request permission to continue his association with the group. Cabales asked how many students Giron had at his academy. Giron answered six. Cabales replied that it was not enough for him to travel and teach in Tracy. Giron said he didn't want to teach, he just wanted to be part of the arnis escrima association. Cabales and Giron walked away and Giron continued to teach at his club in Tracy while Cabales continued to teach in Stockton.

Giron would still visit grandmaster Cabales at the serrada academy to help and demonstrate his style of larga mano cabarron (new) arnis escrima. In 1973, Giron relocated his residences and his arnis escrima club to Stockton. Grandmaster Giron is still active and teaches class for all of those that would like to train in the Filipino arts.

Q: It has recently been stated on the Internet escrima sites that Leo Giron studied escrima from Angel Cabales. Also that Leo's own system, estilo de fondo, is nothing but a copy of Cabales' serrada system. Is there any truth to this?

A: Well first of all, it is sad that people are willing to make this kind of effort to try and discredit others, especially our fathers in the arts who have endured so many

A ONE ON ONE INTERVIEW

hardships and struggles. It's somewhat ironic that the people that say such things are similar to the type of people that verbally and in some cases physically assaulted our forefathers during they're early years here in America. I will say that I will not bring myself down to this level and try to justify remarks of this nature. I feel in most cases that many escrima groups are making great progress in bridging the past with fellowship and goodwill to all in an effort to unite all Filipino arts. I will not be a part of those who in some cases have not met or played with either grandmaster Cabales or grandmaster Giron, for any significant amount of time, to make such remarks or judgments, but yet are willing to plant a seed of evil. In short, focus and energy should be spent on promoting the arts, not tearing them down.

Q: What is your opinion about mixing Escrima styles?

A: Mixing Escrima systems can be confusing for everyone. It has been the teachings of grandmaster Giron that learning other Escrima styles can help you to understand the Filipino arts and see the big picture. But, as a teacher or student of the Filipino arts, you must always identify with the styles you are playing. Meaning that if you are teaching a certain style of escrima, you must always let your students know what style you are now teaching. You must also acknowledge the styles and masters of those systems.

As for effectiveness, it can be like mixing oil and vinegar. On the other hand, mixing styles can prove to be an effective combination that is quite deadly.

Q: is that why you find many systems with long, medium and short range technques?

A: It is a natural survival apporach to combat. The founders of the methods understood that in combat you have to be prepared to react at different ranges, therefore thye implemented tehcniques suitable to those three ranges of fighting. It was never an approach to "mix" styles but a logical way of prepparing themselves for all-range

TONY SOMERA: In His Own Words

combat. In some wasy we can say that the mentally they used was very open, a very eclectic way to look at combat and simply using and develop thise things that were required to survive.

Q: How can a practitioner increase his understanding of the spiritual aspect of the art?

A: Certainly, if you are practicing an art, you are already studying the spiritual aspect of the art. From the time you step on the floor to train you begin to sense or pick up certain characteristics of your teacher and fellow students. Watch what is taking place around you as you train. Be aware of how your teacher is teaching the art; be aware of how you and your fellow students demonstrate the art. Do your research and ask questions. Try to learn more about your art's history and culture and by all means ask your teacher questions.

Q: Let's talk a little bit about the philosophy of martial arts. What it would be the final statatement you would give to your students?

A: I always enjoyed the Japanese philosophy about martial arts and reading Zen works inspired me to understand the "mind of the warrior". Takuan was a Zen priest that wrote the book "The Record of Miraculous Immovable Wisdom" and was cosidered the spiritual guide of the legendary Miyamoto Musashi.

When he was on his deathbed. Takuan was requested to give the final instructions to his students and followers. He just wrote one single word: "dream".

For him life was a long continuous dream and we are all pulled into the things of our daily lives. He knew that. In a different moment in time, but the distractions of life were basically the same. It is important to go back to the the "basics of life" and see what is important, not letting ourselves to be distracted by the brings daily life bring to us.

It is important to go back to the real meaning of martial arts....to what Takuan called the "sword of life".

A ONE ON ONE INTERVIEW

Q: You like to mention that making "mistakes" is a necessary evil in the world of martial arts and in lite itself. Would you elaborate on that?

A: Even when we do our best, we still make mistakes. It seems to be that people are afraid or embarrased of making mistakes in anything they do. Making mistakes is a "neccesary evil" for growth. We have to respond correctly to out mistakes because they are another form of learning. A mistake is only a mistake when we do not pay attention to it and try to correct it so we will eventually repeated again. Tere is nobody else to blame for our mistakes in training or in life. Therefore, it is important to take these things or techniques we do in life and training and work hard to make them our best assets or our best techniques. Be positive and learn how to make mistakes "correctly".

Q: Martial arts styles in general are always evolving and changing with the times, how do you see the Giron Escrima method evolve in the future?

TONY SOMERA: In His Own Words

"Even when we do our best, we still make mistakes. It seems to be that people are afraid or embarrassed of making mistakes in anything they do. Making mistakes is a "necessary evil" for growth."

A ONE ON ONE INTERVIEW

A: I am not qualified to speak about other styles of methods and their evolution over time but I can speak for the mehtod developed by Grandmaster Emeritus Leo Giron. The Giron Escrima methods has basicaly all the tools a practitioner needs to be efficient in any range. The system not only has the techniques and the training methods but also a deep philosophical base attached to it. It is important to move forward but not to forget that "the chairs on a dinning table are on the floor and not on top of the table."

It is not about reinventing the wheel, move things around and create a "technical chop-suey'…that is not evolution. Many people simply to that to ceate "their own" and basically they are not doing anything new. Everything that they come up with… it is already there.

It is more important to go deeper into the understanding and application of what it is already there in the style than trying to recreate things that are already created.

TONY SOMERA: In His Own Words

The only reason to try to "reinvent the wheel" is a lack of understanding.

Q: Martial arts are becoming "sports" nowadays. How do you see the sportive aspect of Escrima in the current times?

A: Sports are an important part of our society and help us to communicate and enjoy things we love in a group environment. Escrima was not developed as a sport but as an art of war. That is why it is a "blade art". We have today Escrima/Arnis/Kali tournaments but we can not loose sight of fact that one solid precise hit with a blade means dead while in a tournament you ca get hit five or six times and points are scored but this is not true if you have to protect your life. In short, it is good to enjoy the sportive aspects but we should train for "real" combat and "real" actions and reactions to a life threading situation.

Q: What do you think is the unique characteristic of the art of Escrima?

A: I think versatility. Escrima teaches you how to deal with attacks based on the angle they are delivered…and not in the specifics of the tool used for the attack. You

A ONE ON ONE INTERVIEW

can understand the peculiarities of the attack and not enter too much in the details of the weapon. It is true that the weapon used determines some aspects of the defense that you are going to use but the overall understanding is based on the angle of attack and this single principles streamline many of the options we have to react against an attacl.

Q: When the art becomes a "way of life"?

A: It is when we apply those ethical and moral principles that we find in the arts to our daily life that the art enters in a different dimension. You learn about the resect for life, the relationships with your fellow Esdrima brothers, the kindness found in those relationships, the value of the history of the art and its usefulness in our modern society. The moral and ethical principles become a "guideline" for your life and therefore the art becomes a "way of life".

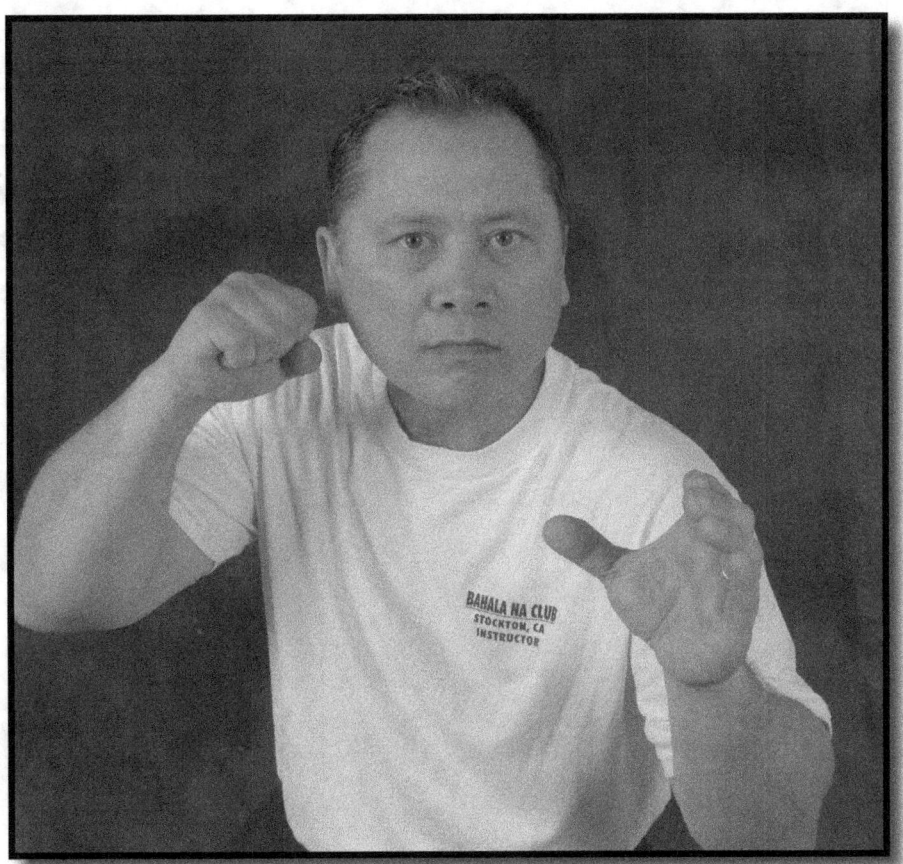

TONY SOMERA: In His Own Words

A ONE ON ONE INTERVIEW

Q: What are your thoughts on the future of the arts?

A: We are in a time of history that is so very important. With many — if not all — of the masters that have paved the way for us passing away, our generation will now need to set the standards for the next generation of practitioners. We must continue to carry on the arts of our forefathers. We must be the ones that will teach and tell the stories of the ancient ones. The stories of the manongs that were experts in the Filipino arts that came to this country to seek a better opportunity and to have a better life. We must never forget all of the wonderful experiences that we had shared with them so that our experiences will be those that will follow in tracing our footsteps. The most wonderful gift I can give will be the teachings of my teacher to the next generation of practitioners so that our forefather's hardships that they had to endure will not be in vain.

Q: How do you want to be remembered?

A: That is a difficult question to answer when I am still alive...but I guess it is the only time when I can answer it. Kidding aside, I'd like to be remembered first as a family man. A man who worked hard with dignity to serve his family and his community. I want to be remembered as someone who dedicated his efforts to preserve the legacy of the Filipino culture and art of Escrima; someone loyal to his believes and to those whom believed in me. And as a martial artists I want to leave the legacy of Giron Esrima for the generations to come. Grandmaster Leo Giron was not only a great Escrima leader but an honest and loving human being and I want his legacy to stay alive.

GRANDMASTER SOMERA'S WRITINGS

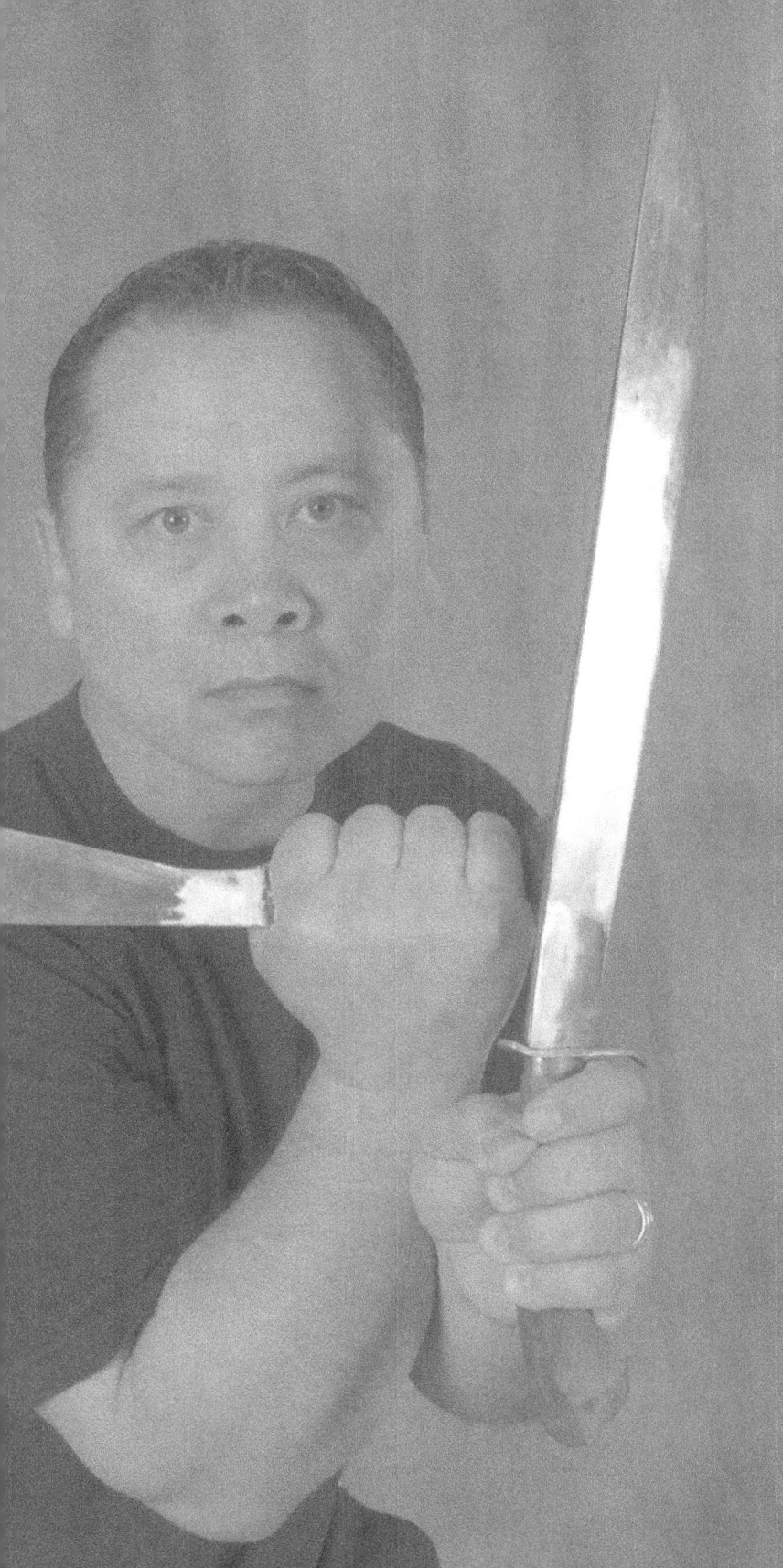

TONY SOMERA: In His Own Words

COMING TO AMERICA

In the mid 1560's the Philippine Islands became a territory of Spain. During the nearly 333 years of Spanish occupation the Philippines would go through many small revolutions in an attempt to regain their freedom from the Spanish imperialism. For instance in 1892 a small body of young Filipino leaders secretly banded together and started to form and organize other groups of Filipino patriots with the aim to begin a coordinated struggle to retake their native homeland. This was the beginning of the Katipunan. The Katipunan was a Philippine revolutionary society founded by anti-Spanish Filipinos in Manila in 1892, which aimed primarily to gain independence from Spain by any means necessary including armed revolution. The word 'Katipunan" means simply "association" but the complete official name of this revolutionary force was "Kataas-taasang, Kagalang-galangang Katipunan" or, "The most high and honorable society of children of the Nation".

In order to gain membership to this secret society it was first thought out by the leader Andres Bonifacio to recruit within a "triangle" system. The triangle system of recruiting would start as such, the tip of the triangle would know the other two members, but the other two did not know each other. However, at the end of a year the system was abolished after proving to be too clumsy and complicated. A new system of initiation was then adopted which was modeled after existing Masonic rites. The new way to become a member of the Katipunan would be through completion of a set of initiation rites, resembling those of established Masonic organizations, which were created to test the applicant's courage, patriotism and loyalty.

After many years of bloody struggle the revolution was a limited success. Freedom was won from the Spanish but only with help from the United States. Once the Spanish left the continuous US presence became resented by many Filipinos and the relationship that was once helpful for the Philippines turned violent. It was only after a final short but bloody war with the United States of America, and not until well after the turn of the 20th century, that the Philippines would gain her independence. The US presence remained, but at an acceptable level for both the US and the Filipinos.

Mainly for economic and social reasons many young Filipino men began to travel to the United States beginning in the 1906 to 1932. This first wave of young Filipino men that came from the Philippines to America were truly sons of

GRANDMASTER SOMERA'S WRITINGS

the Revolution. This early and sustained influx of Filipino culture set the stage for Filipino inclusion in what would become the thousands of young men that would make up and be counted as America's greatest generation, the WWII generation. These men came with a hopeful attitude and the revolutionary experience of life to make their dreams into reality.

However, life in American soon proved to be equally as difficult to the life they left because of discriminatory feelings within America for these young Filipino men.

Filipinos that travel to American would find out that life would not always be a land of opportunity but could be a land of cruelties and racism. But much like their forefathers of the Katipunan these young men would not be easily defeated. They wanted

to belong to a greater America. One of the ways they were able to gain access to American society was to recreate and partake in established international fraternal organizations by banding together and forming their own groups of Filipino Masonic Lodges.

These Filipino Masonic groups formed their own secret social and society groups, with a focus on the working classes. Within these groups the Filipino immigrants created enclaves of brotherhood, friendship and community. To this day there are still these same Filipino Masonic lodges that still carry out the same rituals and ceremonies that were practiced during the days of the Katipunan. These were the young men, in the Masonic groups, who would train and pass on behind the locked doors of the temple the martial arts of the revolution; the warrior arts of the Katapunan.

And out of these Masonic orders would grow the many modern day Filipino Martial Art Icon's that Martial Art giant Guro Dan Inosanto would seek out. His discovery revealed a hot bed of Filipino Martial art masters residing in his own hometown of Stockton California. Men like Angle Cabalas, Joe Papaco, Leo M. Giron, Jesus Corallas, Juanito Lacoste, Pasqual Ovales, Gilbert Tenio Victorino Ton, the eldest at 109 years young, and many more, who had made the journey from the Philippines to the US for the chance of a better life for themselves and their families.

TONY SOMERA: In His Own Words

GROWING UP IN AMERICA

The years 1906 through 1932 saw the first wave of young Filipino men coming to the United States mainly to work as farm laborers. These young men came to America with little or no money with them and only what they were wearing as they left home in the Philippines, with maybe one change of clothing. As they went to their new job's most did not know exactly what they really would be doing in the farms and fields of central California and other US agricultural centers. Most did not know anything about asparagus, celery or lettuce, but through hard work they would help create the agricultural giant of the Central California Valley, including the San Joaquin valley and the Sacramento-San Joaquin River Delta, that even now feeds much of the US and world population. However, it was not an easy path by any means for these early Filipino emigrants.

In their quest for a better life many young Filipino men saw America as the land of opportunity. After the Philippine Revolution of 1896-1898, and the Philippine-American War of 1899-1902 the country became a recruiting station for the US labor market and was inundated with labor contractors sent by the large agriculture facilities in the US. Filipino labor was in very high demand by the large farm companies because of the hard work ethic held and demonstrated by Filipinos. Unfortunately, many of the American labor contractors turned out to be unscrupulous business men and many young men were lured into labor contracts which were often unfair and discriminatory. The sales pitch made telling of excellent working conditions and of the great wealth to be made were, at best, misleading promises that did not materialize once the relocation from the Philippines was finished and the work in the US was started. For instance, often the migrating worker had to take a loan from the contractor just to make the move to the US which automatically put the worker in debt to the contractor. The average labor contract would last 2 to 4 years, but often times much longer because in the small print the contract made the labor last, "until their debt was paid".

Many of these young men would come to America with little or no money with them and only what there were wearing and maybe one change of clothing. As they would go to their newfound job's they would be unaware of what they would really be doing. Most if not all of them do not know what was asparagus, celery or lettuce.

GRANDMASTER SOMERA'S WRITINGS

Harvesting Asparagus would be the training ground for them to master their Martial Arts skills with the very tool they used every day to cut and harvest the asparagus, the Asparagus Knife. Depending on the height of the man, the type of soil and what type of asparagus would determine the type of asparagus knife. The knife has a short wooden handle that is connected to a steel rod with average length of 24 inches that ends in flat, razor sharp tip. The ringing sound of steal on steal could be heard far off in the hidden corners of the asparagus camps as the secret escrima masters played the ancient Philippine warrior arts of their homeland away from prying eyes. You would be able to hear the clanging of metal against metal, thrusting, poking, sounds of the air being cut and hands parrying and slapping their town mates hand to the side. What is very common is for any of these young Filipino men would do is too be very quiet about their knowledge of what they knew about martial arts. If others would know many times they would be challenged or if other cultures would find out they would be an easy target of a group fight in which was very easy anyway because of their race.

Other times were more simple and quiet. These young men would stay in their camp, playing cards, washing clothes, or telling stories of back home in the Philippines. They would tell stories about their families as lonely young men will often do.

After working long hard hours during the week in the fields many of the young Filipinos would travel into Stockton, California to visit their friends or town mates and to try to find a little entertainment. This common search for community involvement or just the joys of "big city" life were the seeds of the "Little Manila" experience to come.

Also, in later years many of these same men would rush to join the US Army during the out- break of World War II to help recover their native home land of the Philippine Islands. They would become heroes and return to America to start a new life and take a second chance of becoming part of American society.

TONY SOMERA: In His Own Words

DREAMS COME TRUE

On April 1, 1942 the First Filipino Infantry was formed in San Luis Obispo. Every student of history knows of the bombing of Pearl Harbor, Hawaii on December 7, 1941 but few know that on the next day, December 8, 1941 the Imperial Japanese also bombed the US and Filipino forces in Manila Bay, Philippines. The attack was very effective and devastating for the allied forces and the foreign invaders soon took over the Philippines forcing the American and Philippine military out of the Philippines to relocate to other strong holds in the hope to live to fight another day. These events would inspire Filipinos living in America to petition for the right to serve in the United States military. After a hard political fight on January 2, 1942 President Franklin Roosevelt signed a law revising the selective service act. Filipinos were now able to join the U.S. Armed forces and many thousands of Filipino volunteers would rush to join the U.S. Armed forces in hopes of help in the recapture of their native homeland the Philippine Islands. There were so many Filipino recruits rushing to enlist that orders were given to form the famous 1st Filipino Infantry Regiment that was formed in Salinas California on July 13, 1942. After this Filipino recruits continued to volunteer in increasing numbers, so much so that the 2nd Filipino Infantry Regiment was formed on November 21, 1942 at Camp Cooke California. During one of the largest mass naturalization ceremony at Camp Beale, California in 1943 Filipino American soldiers from the 1st Filipino Infantry Regiment were sworn in as United States Citizens. Although it would fulfill a lifetime dream of becoming an American citizen for many of these young Filipino men, citizenship came at a price. They were inducted into the military, naturalized as US citizens, and then off to war they went! The price was high but none flinched from their duty to their country, the United States, or to their homeland, the Philippines.

It was out of these thousands of members of the 1st and 2nd Filipino Infantry Regiments that then commander and leader of the Pacific theater General Douglas Macarthur would hand select men to form a small group of secret elite commando group. These commandos were assigned to send back vital information setting the foundation for the retaking of the Philippine Islands. This secret group of elite fighting men was known as the 978th Signal Service Company. All became highly skilled in jungle survival, jungle fighting and were experts in the Filipino Martial arts of Escrima, Arnis and Kali. These special fighting men were dropped off

GRANDMASTER SOMERA'S WRITINGS

behind enemy lines by secret submarines nearly one year before any American soldier landed on Philippine soil. Their assignment was top secret and has only recently been declassified. Their mission objectives were so secret and important that even at the time their orders were to "take no prisoners" in any encounter with the enemy. Bahala Na was there slogan, "come what may".

The secret commandos would travel through the jungle and collect vital information such as the location of the Japanese military and the intricate troop movements. The commandos would also relay back to base their estimates of Japanese supplies and send eye witness accounts of how the enemy was treating the local citizens, all in an effort to prepare the US intelligence forces and military units for the bloody battles to win back the Philippine islands.

Specifically, the 978th Signal Service members would send back this needed information through Morse code to Allied Headquarters. Often the commandos would encounter the enemy and be forced to use their own cultural martial art of Escrima Arnis Kali to defend themselves from by swinging their bolo knifes or machetes to silently cut down the enemy forces. No American commando could allow himself to be captured because this would be proof for their enemy that American commandos were already on Philippine soil preparing for the invasion by General Macarthur, the 1st and 2nd Filipino Infantry Regiment, and the entire US invasion force.

When the final invasion came it was a great allied success in no small part because of the efforts of these men from the 978th Signal Company. These highly skilled commandos trained in the Filipino Martial Art of Escrima Arnis and Kali were the first of their kind in American Military history.

These first generation Filipinos came to America and set the standard for future generations. During WWII many earned their right to citizenship and many made the ultimate sacrifice for that right. These men were proud Filipino Americans and also proud Filipino Fraternal Lodge members like Leo M. Giron, Leon Ancheta, Secundio Bucol, Victorino Castillo, Raynaldo Domingo, Antonio Dizon Felicitas, Monico Luis, Juan Peralta, Ventura Serquinia, Cornelio Supnet to name only a few of thousands that were there. These were some of the men who became known in time as "America's Greatest Generation".

TONY SOMERA: In His Own Words

PLAYING THE ART IN SECRET

At the end of World War II Filipino American soldiers came home to America with a new sense of pride, honor and dignity. These proud Filipino Americans came back to their new home wanting to forget about the horrors of war. They wanted to start their life over by beginning families and adjusting to civilian life. Being members of the United States Military and now being American Citizens seemed to fulfill their dreams of becoming "real Americans".

Many returned to their hometowns looking for their town mates and friends.

One of the most familiar ways to return to normal life was to return to their secret lodges and fraternal orders. The hub of all of this was centered in Stockton, California because it had the largest Filipino population in America. At the time Stockton, California was known across the United States as "Little Manila". It was common knowledge that if you were Filipino living in Stockton, California you would belong to one of the big three Filipino Fraternal Orders; the Caballeros de Dimas Alang lodge, the Gran Oriente Filipino lodge or the largest and most powerful Legionarios del Trabajo in America lodge. These Filipino lodges were groups of Filipinos Fraternal Orders that open their doors to anyone who would like to be a part of the Filipino culture and heritage. They all practice social equality, brotherhood and sisterhood. But one of the most interesting facts about these groups are that most of their members were experts in the Filipino Martial art of Escrima, Arnis and Kali. During my research I learned that the founders of the Filipino lodges could all remember the times after their monthly meetings when some of these experts would go into the secret temple behind locked doors and play their cultural martial art. Many of them agreed that their training was fun but also intense. From boxing (that was adopted by Americans in the early 1900's and is now known as western style boxing) or bare hand vs. bare hand, moving on to short pocket palm stick to dagger, then advancing to short stick to long stick, many styles were played within the lodge. For the World War II veterans that were experts in the use of the bolo knife, they would play with the short and long bolo knives. If it was asparagus season many of these experts would bring their asparagus knives to spar using the tools of their trade. Many of these Manongs mentioned that there would always be a guard next to the door so that no one that was not invited too these sparing matches could enter the training area.

Even a lodge member would need to have several keys to enter these highly secret training sessions. The first required key was to have a personal invitation

GRANDMASTER SOMERA'S WRITINGS

from someone already accepted into the training circle. The second required key was knowledge of the secret knock. Finally, the third key was knowledge of the secret password.

These training or playing sessions would mostly be friendly competitions, and they would always be between members of lodges from the same body of their mother fraternal orders. Very rarely would members from other outside lodges be allowed to mix into a training circle. Members such as Leo M. Giron, Joe Pacpaco, Victorino Ton, to name a few, were always there after the meetings to share their village's martial art. These martial skills were held so highly secretive by the practitioners that many of their own family members did not know of their martial art abilities. To understand these types of secret training sessions you would need to keep in mind that the base and foundation of these meetings were much like the secret meetings of their lodge. It was also understood that to play this secret martial art would also be dangerous for these men because if they were discovered they would be open to challenge which could easily lead to injury or death for the combatants. During these times it was well known that if you were to brag about your ability of Filipino martial arts there would always be someone out there who would not be as open to share and not open to the practice of social equality, brotherhood and sisterhood. The common slogan was that if you open your mouth or brag about your ability in the Filipino martial art that someone would "shove the stick down your throat".

Bragging was not the normal practice of lodge brothers or sisters. In fact, not until groundbreaking research in the late 1960's would the world know of these experts in the Filipino martial arts. It would be through the hard investigative work of world-renowned martial artist Guro Dan Inosanto that the world would know the identity of some of these Filipino martial art icons.

Today many of these original Filipino lodge members have since joined our heavenly father. But, you need to ask the question these days do these Filipino Fraternal orders still honor the memory of our forefathers through the practice of social equality, brotherhood and sisterhood? The answer is a resounding yes. But are there still those secret groups of Filipino lodge members who practice the deadly Filipino Martial Arts of our forefathers? Well, that answer is simple too, but no one will give the answer because those secret warriors who truly practice the arts will never tell.

TONY SOMERA: In His Own Words

WHAT HAS BEEN LEARNED?

During the many years of our forefathers struggles and sacrifices they have paved the way in which we now know as our fathers of Filipino martial arts, this that bridges our generation to our fathers generation and our heritage to our fathers heritage and our fathers way of life to our own way of life starts a new chapter in Filipino Martial Arts. All that has been pass down to us, the many hours of learning, the many hours of listening, the many ours of loving the very art that has influenced Americas greatest generation. We now are the caretakers of this ancient way of life and there ancient martial art.

Because of our interest and the wellness to try and understand our own culture. We need to ask the question and try to bring the knowledge and history of what our fathers had to endure. This was not an easy task; our fathers did not want to reveal the cruelties of a nation. They remain quite, hard working, proud, passionate, dedicated to their families, dedicated to their beliefs, and dedicated to their commitments. Many of them would say that they were also the "best looking"; the best dancers and many would admit the best lovers but very rarely would they brag about there skill in the Filipino martial arts.

What would we learned from these super men. Men that was thrown into manhood after leaving there families at such a young age, many in there teens to chase there dreams of being Americans, of being wealthy, being successful and being of family.

When we would call them Uncle, Manong (elder), Ninog (godfather) and now today we are the Uncle's, we are now the Manong's (elders) and we are now the Ninog's (godfathers). As time has quickly advanced forward we are thrush into a new role for us but an old role for our Uncle's. They made it look so easy, their movements like swan's that move in the water effortless. A role in which we would never have seen myself, a role in which we are now the elders and we are the Guro's the Manong's and now the Ninog's (godfathers).

Through the Filipino martial arts they have taught us our history and our culture. By teaching us the techniques of self-defense they teach us the reasons why we call it a roof block or inside block. This culture of the art is the culture of a people. In order to learn more about our forefathers we learn the Filipino martial arts. So we take the time to listen, learn and love.

GRANDMASTER SOMERA'S WRITINGS

In order to continue this legacy of our forefather we must open our hearts to share what they have guarded by our forefathers for so many years, this the art that was held in such high regards and the highest of secrecy even there family members did not even know of the highly skilled art that they possessed.

We now have the role of sharing the art with those that would like to learn more about the greatest generation. We are the caretakers of Filipino martial arts this culture of a proud people and the teaching of our history that is deeply rooted by the soil of our forefathers known as the ancient ones. How do we do this, by the same tools our teachers had taught us, through the martial arts? We will tell the stories as they were told to us we teach the Filipino martial art of self-defense as they were taught to us. And as we teach the art of self-defense as we teach our history and culture through the stories that we were taught. How do we do this, easy one movement at a time, one story at a time, one chapter of history at a time? This until it is time for our students to continue and to fulfill the legacy in which they will now be the new uncles, manong's and ninog's they will become the new legacy of Filipino martial arts, until it is time for the cycle will continue and repeat. So who is next? Who will be up for the challenge? Who will take on the responsibility, who will be the next? Will this be your legacy?

TONY SOMERA: In His Own Words

ESCRIMA LODGE

Filipino Martial Arts have been around for many generations and are as old as the history of the Philippines. Because of the deep cultural stresses from the Spanish occupation of the islands, the Filipino Martial Arts became a hidden and a secret treasure for the practitioners who had to practice the arts in secret. Since 1596, our forefathers were forced to practice the art by moonlight or candlelight to avoid persecution or even death at the hands of the Spanish regime. Later, the secret Filipino Martial Arts were used by the revolutionary forces and helped to liberate the Philippines from the Spanish who occupied the Philippines for more than 330 years.

The revolutionary society was and is now known as the Katipunan. It was a secret society organized along Masonic lines; through skillful use of politics and warfare on varying fields of battle, it achieved its desire and obtained independence from Spain. The Katipunan would be the model and catalyst for later Filipino organizations to come, as Filipinos once again were forced to band together for strength and support in the new fields of America. Here, the determination and power gained through knowledge of the Filipino Martial Arts will again show its usefulness in liberating the Filipinos who keep the secrets of the arts.

After independence from Spain, and throughout the colonization by America, or what was called the new beginning of an American territory, the Philippines became a natural recruiting ground for large American labor corporations looking for a cheap labor source to work in the fields of the U.S. In the early 1900s, for many reasons, these offers of work at first appeared very attractive to young Filipino men who were looking to create a new and better life for themselves in a new country. But the rewards were long in coming and hard to win. The recruited laborers did backbreaking stoop labor for low wages for years and suffered greatly to create the bright future of their dreams. The labor corporations, in order to maximize the profits from the field work, would force the Filipino laborers to live in substandard housing in labor camps that had little or no running water or heat during the winter. These young Filipino men also would face racism and prejudice in order to maintain their dreams of a life of riches in the newfound home of America. However, through industriousness and perseverance Filipinos thrived in the new environment and began a journey to make themselves the equal of any citizens of the United States. For many of these first-generation Filipinos, the beginning of the journey started at El Dorado Street (the street of gold) in Stockton, California.

GRANDMASTER SOMERA'S WRITINGS

As the different Filipino groups began to solidify and occupy the area of Stockton, many social obstacles became obvious to them. For instance, Filipinos could note vote or own property at this time in the U.S. As in the old days of the Katipunan, they decided to form many different clubs, associations, organizations, and Masonic lodges that would be a unique feature of Filipino American society. The lodges became a place to conduct social affairs and business that the first- generation Filipinos could not conduct in other ways within the society of the time.

The "Big Three" Secret Filipino fraternal orders, as many Filipino would refer to them, were the Caballeros de Dimas Alang Lodge, Grand Oriente Filipino Lodge, and the strongest and most powerful lodge, the Legionarios del Trabajo Lodge. The first of these lodges was started in 1924 in San Francisco. And on February 11, 1927, the Francisco Daguhoy Lodge was formed in Stockton California, which by that time was home to thousands of Filipinos.

Behind the locked and guarded doors, many of these first-generation Filipinos would "play" or train in their ancient Filipino Martial Art of Escrima Arnis. It was common in the early days that these young Filipinos would spend a Sunday afternoon after their secret lodge meetings to play and practice sharing the Martial Arts of their forefathers.

After the outbreak of World War II, many of these Filipino men would enlist into the United States Army to serve and fight to retake their native homeland the Philippine Islands. More than 12,000 Filipino men would join and create the 1st and 2nd Filipino Infantry. Out of these 12,000 men, General Douglas MacArthur selected nearly 900 to serve as his secret commandos; one of these men was Sergeant Leo M. Giron of Bahala Na Martial Arts Association. He would credit his membership in the Filipino Lodge, and his continued Martial Arts practice there, with much of his success in his military roll which helped to liberate his homeland.

It has been my pleasure to also be a member of this same Filipino Lodge for nearly 30 years. My Illustrious Brother Leo M. Giron, who became the founder of the Bahala Na Filipino Martial Arts Association after the war and his lodge brother, my father, Illustrious Brother Chester S. Somera Sr., both sponsored me to join this ancient brotherhood that maintains an active lodge to this day. In the Legionarios del Trabajo Lodge of Little Manila, Stockton, California, well over 100 years has gone by, with the secret rituals and ceremonies continuing within the lodge and through its members. To this day, you can find first-generation Manongs who remain after their regular lodge meetings to visit upstairs behind locked and guarded doors. You can hear laughing, talking, and sticks clanging as the ancient and secret Filipino Martial Art continues strong. As with the ancient Katipunan, the Filipino Lodge offers a model to the community and shows the new generation how to properly maintain the commitment and dignity forged by practicing the secret Filipino Martial Arts in the Escrima Lodge.

TONY SOMERA: In His Own Words

THE HIDDEN TREASURE

It has been more than 30 years since Dan Inosanto introduced the world to the Filipino Martial Arts, and it took Guro Dan nearly 15 years before that to learn the martial arts of his ancestors. Encouragement from his late teacher and good friend Sifu Bruce Lee too seek out his roots of martial arts and to learn of the many unsung master in the arts was the mission of young Inosanto. Without a doubt, his groundbreaking book, The Filipino Martial Arts as taught by Dan Inosanto, would open the door and would be the reference book and inspirational guide for many students and teachers to seek out the masters and the many different styles of Filipino Martial Arts that Inosanto featured in this now hard to find collector's book. This powerful book was a wealth of information that exposed thousands of readers to an art that was lost from Filipino society here in America. This book truly would inspire countless readers to research further and to seek additional information on the Filipino Martial Arts.

The names of humble men that the world has never heard of before would become Filipino Martial Arts icons, a kind of Superstars to America and eventually to the world. These men also would become role models, father figures, and men who would change the life destinies of thousands upon thousands of people and would find a new found respect for the Filipino community and its hidden Martial Arts.

The Filipino Martial Art treasures Inosanto uncovered for America and the world would be men by the names of Pepe Montano Arca and Vincent Arca, escrima instructors who came to the Hawaiian Islands and eventually would accompany the first Filipino immigrants who, without knowing it, would kept the art alive:

Pepe Montno Arca was Inosanto's grandfather; Master Pedro Apilado was known as one of the top fighters and would serve as head referee in the Hawaiian Islands in the days when full contact stick fighting was done without armor; Master Apilado also was a student under the great champion of the Northern Philippines, Santiago Toledo; the famous Canete family would have the largest escrima school in the Philippines; Grand Master Angel Cabales, considered the man responsible for the exposure of escrima to the American public, was most effective with the short stick and was a true master of the art; Master Regino Ellustrisimo a master in

GRANDMASTER SOMERA'S WRITINGS

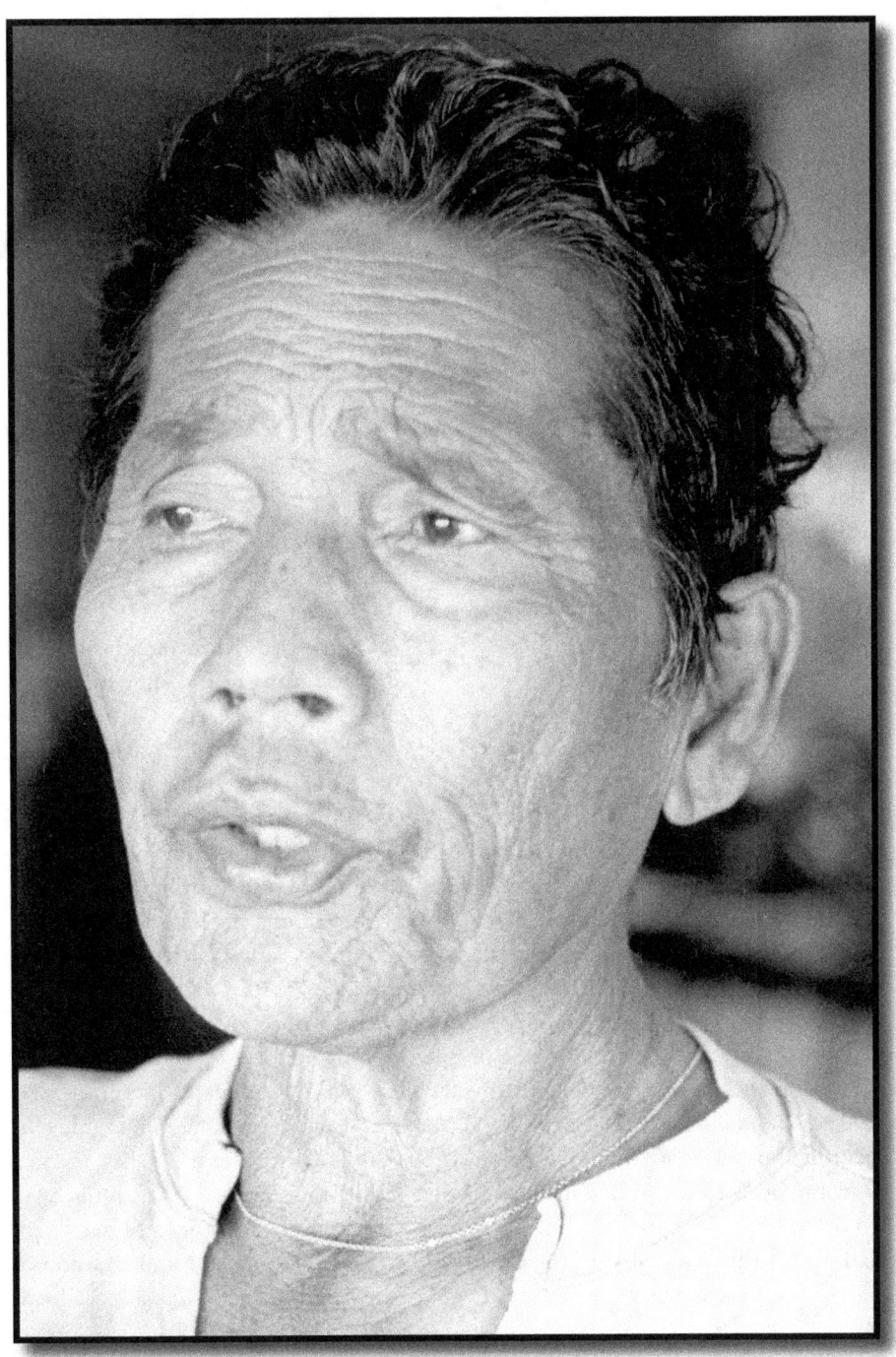

TONY SOMERA: In His Own Words

the Bohol method of escrima; Grand Master Leo M. Giron, a man with a wealth and knowledge of the combative art of arnis escrima whose combat proven style was tested during World War II for more than a year in the jungles of the Philippines (Insoanto would consider Leo Giron to be his second father).

Also, Grand Master Juanito Lacoste, considered by Inosanto to be the most well-rounded escrimador and a master of stick, dagger, long blade, and empty hands; Grand Master Ben Largusa, the most all-around Filipino Kali martial artist, according to Inosanto, and a student of the great Grand Master Floro Villabrille, champion of countless matches in the Philippines and Hawaii; Master Pasqual Ovales, the grandson of the great Santiago Toledo, a master in the Toledo-Collando style of escrima that uses the long stick and "escala" (stroking pattern) of training; Grand Master Braulio Pedoy, who taught escrima but also the awareness of the history of the Filipino martial art and culture; Master Narrie Babao, who holds the title of champion in the first weapons sparring tournament held in the United States; Grand Master Lucky Lucay Lucay, whose expertise is in "Sikara (Filipino Foot Fighting) and Panatukan (Filipino Boxing).

Also on the list are Master Dentoy Revillar, senior student of Grand Master Cabales and the first to train with both Cabales and Giron, making him highly efficient in both the short and long stick methods, and an organizer in the first escrima academy open to the public in the United States; Grand Master Jack Santos, who serves as an advisor to the Filipino Kali Academy in Torrance; Master Max Sarmiento, a man gifted with the use of empty hands, dagger, and knives, who was one of the first, along with his wife Lynn, to help organize the Cabales academy,

GRANDMASTER SOMERA'S WRITINGS

the first open to the general public in the United States; Grand Master Telesporo Subing Subing, an expert in the Moro style and double stick style of the Southern Philippines; Grand Master Sam Tendencia, who trained under the great Deogracias Tipace in the Philippines and is expert in the art of Filipino nerve pinching and Hilot (massage); Grand Master Gilbert Tenio, who trained in many Filipino arts and was founder of the Tenio Dequedas system in Stockton, California; Grand Master Floro Villabrille of Hawaii, known as the undefeated champion in countless escrima and kali matches in the Philippines and Hawaii; And Grand Master Viliabrille, who at that time was the head of the Kali organization.

Add to the group Grand Master Richard Bustillo, who during that time was Inosanto's training partner and also was responsible for promoting and preserving the Filipino Martial Arts and Jeet Kune Do; Ed Parker, Inosanto's instructor in Kenpo karate and in Inosanto's opinion a "true Master," And last but not least the great Sifu Bruce Lee, who was Inosanto's instructor and good friend who guided him to the art of Jeet Kune Do. Under Sifu Lee's tutelage, Inosanto gained the educational eye to find out what was functional in the Martial Arts. Lee also encouraged Inosanto to look for his roots in the arts and to continue until he has found all that is useful.

Guro Dan Inosanto's book The Filipino Martial Arts was so powerful that many individuals followed in his footsteps in researching the Filipino Martial Arts. It is a virtual encyclopedia of unadventured knowledge exposed to the public for our own consumption. Thousands more would experience the art itself and would test the very foundation of the applications of techniques.

After all the research and information publish on the Filipino Martial Arts, you would think that we would have exhausted our wealth of individuals who would play the art of our forefathers. Digging a little deeper in my hometown that once was called "Little Manila" because of the huge Filipino population, Stockton, California, would be the small farming community that to this date still would have a few more hidden treasures.

These men now are the last of their kind, the ancient ones who set the foundation for us to have a better life here in America. These men are still active; some teaching the Filipino Martial Arts and others would be more than happy to demonstrate and tell stories about the many different styles of the Filipino arts.

Jesus Ragail Corales was born in Narvacan, Illocos Sur Philippines on December 25, 1910. Like Giron, Corales arrived in America in 1929. He immediately took a bus from San Francisco to Stockton and would work in the fields and farm labor camps in the San Joaquin valley. Due to his working in the many different Filipino labor camps, he would be exposed to a number of Filipino escrimadors. Corales

TONY SOMERA: In His Own Words

would take the time to play or train in the art after a hard day's work in the fields. He remembers that "after working so hard during the day, in the afternoon, during a cool delta breeze, my town mates and I would sit outside next to the barn away from everyone and play with our asparagus or sticks knives. I can remember the quickness of the weapon but no one would get hurt." Corales' teacher was a man by the name of Hilario Ramolete from Santa Catalina Illocos Sur, Philippines. Corales played the cabaroan or new system of arnis escrima. His specialty was the cinco tero style or five strikes; also the redonda style or circular striking, and close quarter hand-to-hand combat. Corales was a member of the 1st Filipino Regiment and served in the invasion of Lyette, Philippines, during World War II. Of the four in this article, Corales had the most energy. At times, it was difficult to interview him and also play with him because he would keep moving. He would explain his current movement and would already be demonstrating the next movement. His knowledge of the Filipino arts of self-defense is unlimited as his energy to demonstrate it. Corales is also a member of one of the "Big Three" Filipino Lodges of America, The Caballeros de Dimas Alang.

Joe Arruejo Pacpaco was born in Vigan Illocos Sur Philippines on November 24, 1909. He arrived in San Francisco in 1930 on the President Jefferson and went to Stockton by boat through the San Joaquin Delta. As did most of the Filipinos who arrived during this first wave, Pacpaco took his first job cutting celery. He also worked in the many different Filipino farm labor camps in the San Joaquin Valley and occasionally took work in Marysville and Yuba City, California. Pacpaco's teacher was a man by the name of Francisco Realin from Santa Catalina, Philippines. His system of play is the cabaroan or new style of arnis escrima. His style is Larga Mano or long hand/weapon style; he also plays abierta or open body style of arins escrima and he has an empty hand style that is similar to cadena de mano. Pacpaco's Larga mano is different from Leo Giron's larga mano. Pacpaco incorporates the abierta (open) body footwork to his larga mano. Pacpaco's footwork is attributed to his natural open foot movement. Joe Pacpaco has a unique gift of playing. He is left-handed, very graceful and to the point. Pacpaco and Giron would play together in the Giron's basement and at the Filipino Grand Lodge just half a block from both Pacpaco and Giron's house and a block from Inosanto's house. Pacpaco was the person that Giron had in mind to train the "killer" style to Dan Inosanto. Pacpaco is also a life member of the Legionarios Del Trabajo and member of the Worshipful Mabini Lodge with over 60 years of service to the Filipino lodge.

GRANDMASTER SOMERA'S WRITINGS

Victorino Ton was born June 29, 1895, in Lapaz Abra, Philippines. He arrived in Hawaii in 1924 and worked in the pineapple and sugar cane plantations for six years. After completing his work contract in Hawaii he moved on to Stockton, California in 1930. Ton's first job in Stockton was cutting asparagus. To my knowledge, Victorino Ton is the oldest living arnis escrima player in America. At the time of this article Ton was 108 years old and lived at a Filipino lodge in Stockton, enjoying a very simple life, gardening, and playing cards. The first question he had for me was, "why are we so close?" and the second question was, "do I have a longer weapon"? This would lead me to believe he was a cabaroan (new style) escrimador. Ton plays the cinco tero (five strikes) and incorporates blocking and counter striking. He started playing with sticks in the Philippines at the age of 10; this would be 1905. This was without a doubt one of the most fertile times of escrimadors in Philippine history due to the Filipino revolution. Ton is truly a son of the revolution who fought against the Spaniards in the Filipinos' struggle to gain their freedom from Spain. Manong Ton also is a life member of the Legionarios del Trabajo in America and is a member of General Lim lodge with more than 60 years of service to the Filipino lodge.

I would like to mention a few factors that link these four incredible men together.

1. They all came to America during the first wave of Filipinos from the Philippines.
2. They all were farm laborers.
3. They all learned and still practice the Filipino Martial Arts.
4. They all are members of a Filipino Masonic Lodge.
5. They are all from Luzon, Philippines.

Amazingly enough, these hidden treasures are still with us today. My teacher, Grand Master Leo M. Giron, has encouraged to me to seek out the remaining masters or ancient ones of the Filipino arts.

Many thanks to our forefathers like Giron, Corales, Pacpaco, and Ton who endured so many hardships to make our life better. And for those Grand Masters and Masters of the arts, Cabalas, Elustrisimo, Giron, LaCoste, Largusa, Villarille, Canete, Tenio, Pedoy, Tabosa, Ovales, Santos, Revillar, Sarmiento, Lucaylucay, Babao, Paker, Subing Subing, Tendencia, (others that I have not mentioned please forgive me) and the legendary Bruce Lee.

And thanks to people like Inosanto, Bustillo, Lucaylucay, and Dentoy Revillar for helping our generation recognize our Filipino fathers and our heritage. The torch has been passed to us to continue with their work and to ensure the legacy of our forefathers will live on forever.

TONY SOMERA: In His Own Words

SITUATIONS CHANGE

Any fighting style must essentially account for situational changes presented within the evolution of experienced combat. Responsible combatants must evolve and adapt to the acute needs of the battlefield as well as present practitioners of the style with enhanced training opportunities before going into any future conflict. This may be accomplished through diligent practice of the basic fundamentals of the art.

Upon survival of the encounter your mind will review and analyze your own fighting actions after each combat situation. When you do this you will be able to see clearly the changes or alterations that evolved during combat. Every encounter is different from any encounter experience before, and any experience in the future. Each evolution, whether it a new insight into the opponent's state of mind or his physical abilities, use or new type of weaponry, battle in an unknown environment or even subtleties in the elements such as terrain, wind, rain will need to be immediately processed and reviewed in time for complete success. For instance, was the encounter during the day or during the night? What were the successful, or more importantly, the unsuccessful techniques or counters used and witnessed during engagement? This earned knowledge set is the secret knowledge of the warrior and it is this precious knowledge that is passed on between comrades, and among families and between brothers within the combative arts.

One common thread is that by nature the combat situation will change and so will the techniques and applications needed for success. This is because you cannot be certain that you will engage in a well-analyzed situation but must accept the risk of defeat if the wrong technique is implemented. In some situations the style that you will use will be wrong and therefore fatal if you do not evaluate the terrain, the elements and most especially the ability of the opponent and instantaneously adapt.

Evaluation of terrain is important because a failure to recognize the uncertainties of the terrain may result in mission failure and be could easily become fatal. Evaluation of the nature and type of the opponent's weapon is important because if you do not evaluate the threat, for instance, if it is short or long, an edged weapon or a club of hard wood bahi or kamagong, you will not know how to properly counter the weapon. For instance, if he is using a short weapon would it not be to your advantage to use a longer weapon to keep at a safe distance? And would it be to advantage to apply proven techniques on your opponent if he has an edged weapon and you have an edged weapon? For instance, if you have the

GRANDMASTER SOMERA'S WRITINGS

opportunity to block with the back or side of the edged weapon you will be able to maintain the integrity of you weapon and successfully counter the attack. But if you were to block the attack with the sharp edge of your bolo you would surely break or damage your weapon and invite disaster!

Often what we learn in our school or academy is a fixed pattern while the terrain we play on is among the most perfect of conditions. The training floor is free from debris, stones, rocks, roots, shrubs or fallen limbs from trees. The lights in the academy provide good illumination. The environment is dry and free from rain or snow. We are often wearing well-fitted clothing, maybe a special uniform, and eye protection along with form fitting shoes or boots. The most perfect conditions are comfortable and present a fine environment for study. However, such training environment may produce false product from our training so a good practitioner needs to know both the perfect type of terrain or conditions to train and also the most difficult or most dangerous conditions to train. By training under various conditions you will learn to correctly apply your style for combative advantage. This means we should incorporate training outside in the park, or perhaps in the parking lot, or even in a shed or furnished room.

For success we will need to understand and modify our body position and adapt and modify our footwork depending on the terrain. Everything will change under adverse conditions and we need to understand that if we are in a perfect setting to train and the techniques we used, and the footwork and body position used, will change or modify when training in conditions that are dangerous or difficult. Just

TONY SOMERA: In His Own Words

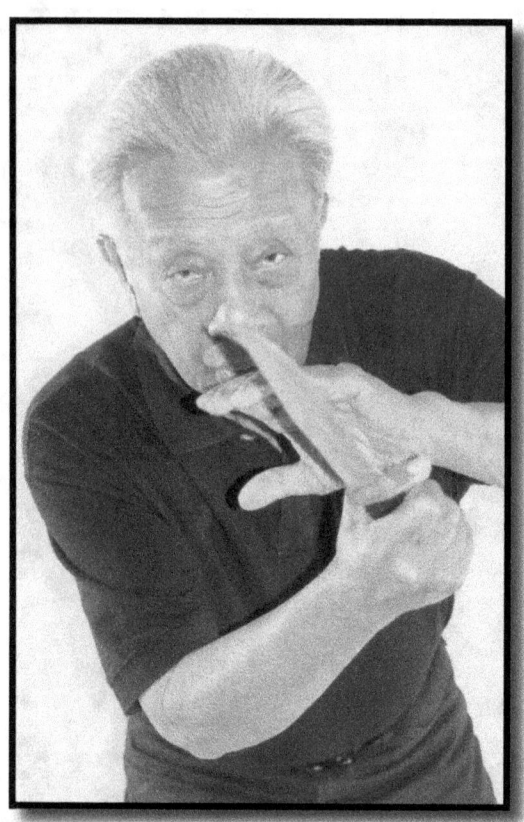

think if you were on a level and even floor, would your stance or footwork change if you were fighting on unnatural terrain or an uneven floor? What if you were sparing in the academy on a nice perfect floor or sparing in the field where there are rocks, potholes, slippery grass or if you were fighting in a muddy field? What if you were fighting on a stairway, on top of a car or over a desk? Will your strategy change? More than likely the answer is yes. So the question then becomes what should you do and how will you handle the different action taken by your opponent under these different conditions? To best train in a traditional way learn the basics from your instructor and follow the direction given. This is the way to learn a style using the basics that your teacher will train you to do. These are known as the basic fundamentals of the art. Then we must take these basics and apply them in every different way possible to gain the widest knowledge of what will work or not work under changing situations. We should keep what works and discard what does not work.

A common goal for many fighting arts, and especially, within the Filipino Martial Arts, is to engrain within each student the ability to the apply techniques under stress. As everyone knows, all techniques work in practice, almost nothing works "for real". Training done between partners works well because we want to see what an "opponent" looks like as they prepare and execute an attack. How must a person stand to deliver an attack? What types of attacks can be delivered from a certain position? The options for the attacker are not unlimited, although in the gap preceding the engagement your mind can easily have you convinced you are dealing with unlimited attack possibilities. By gaining a demonstrated understanding through training of the attack options we may face based on the reasoned

GRANDMASTER SOMERA'S WRITINGS

study of the physical abilities inherent in the attackers position we give ourselves the best chance to counter their actions.

On the other side, by playing the role of an "attacker" we are able to see what a defender does as a counter to our attack. We give ourselves a chance to see the options that the defender may have to counter our own movements, and discover the limits to these counters as well. This give and take, attack and defense, training structure is a helpful tool because as partners we can begin to test each technique for weaknesses in its structure or in our application of it under pressure. Usually, it is the way we apply the technique that is the weak link, but through this partnership of practice we can correct mistakes and perfect our theories and assumptions through trial and error.

By acting out the different roles and situations available in attack and defend modules the student will be more able to adjust to situational changes in combat because he has specifically trained to adapt within his study of the basic fundamental principles of the martial art.

TONY SOMERA: In His Own Words

A HOMECOMING FOR GURO DAN INOSANTO

Once a year Grand Master Tony Somera of Bahala Na Giron Arnis Escrima sponsors one of the most highly shout after martial artist in the world. Guro Dan Inosanto makes his annual seminar stop in Stockton California the birthplace of Filipino Martial Arts in America. But is also unique is that Stockton is the birth place of Guro Dan an icon himself in the world of Martial Arts. From his training of many of the main stream Hollywood movie starts like Danzel Washington in the book of Eli to Guro Dan's many appearances in a number of motion pictures and of course the famous appearance in Martial Art giant Bruce Lee's move such as the game of death to mention.

With many months of preparation it all comes down to a great weekend of lessons of Filipino Martial arts, Filipino History, Filipino Culture and many of Guro Dan's childhood classmates, family and friends that come by to pay there respect to "Danny" or "boom boom" as they would address him. This seminar in Stockton holds a great deal of emotion and memories that every time an old friend or family member drops by a new chapter of history or an old story of Guro Dan's childhood comes out from these meetings. This is what is called priceless by many of those that are lucky enough to be around while this is taking place.

As our first day beginnings I drive to Guro Dan's hotel and pick his assistants and Guro Dan for an early breakfast.

As the first day starts Guro Dan is in perfect form reveling the history of what was at one time the Hub of Filipino's in America, Stockton what is known as "Little Manila" world wide because of the it being the largest population of Filipinos in America, hence the largest population of Filipino Masters of Escrima Arnis Kali. Many of Guro Dan's stories at the breakfast table would be of the early days of growing up in a neighborhood of mixed races in which no one would even pay any attention too. Driving to our destination in which the two day seminar would be held Guro Dan would mention how Stockton has changed and at time how he would get lost driving from street to street trying to recall the names of the streets and remembering how Stockton has grown with houses and stripe malls are now that at one time this was all farm land, farmland that is the riches in the state of Californian. As we park the van many on lookers of students of the Filipino Martial Arts are racing to get into the room in which Guro Dan would conduct

GRANDMASTER SOMERA'S WRITINGS

his seminar. Old friends would meet Guro Dan in the parking lot greeting him and welcome him back home. Hand shakes and hugs with heartfelt greetings and the worlds of Guro Dan, wow this is really Stockton weather, 100 degrees of heat and remembering how it was to work in the fields of Stockton, California. As the day continues Guro Dan's best friend from the old neighborhood and the early days would greet Guro Dan before entering the seminar, Billy, as Guro would call him, they would talk about growing up in the south side of Stockton in which many of the Manong's Escrimadors would live. Filipino Martial Art Icons like Leo M. Giron, Juan Lacoste, Joe Pappaco, Angle Cabales and Victorino Ton. "Billy" would also talk about growing up with "Danny" playing on the same baseball team, basketball team, remembering there old and dear childhood friends and hav-

ing the same teachers. A introduction by Grand Master Tony Somera of the world famous Bahala Na Martial Arts and Giron Arnis Escrima Association and with a hug roar and apologues to greet the home grown and world famous martial artist Guro Dan Inosanto, our formal salute that begins a day of memories of Filipino Martial Arts, Filipino History and a road to remember of Guro Dan's memories of growing up in Stockton California. Guro Dan would start the seminar with several techniques keeping his eye on his childhood friend "Billy" with the anticipation of catching up of many years and of many memories. Guro Dan would work his way through the crowed room helping the attending students until he would meet once

TONY SOMERA: *In His Own Words*

again his childhood best friend "Billy" in which they would talk and laugh about the good old days in Stockton. Guro Dan would then rush back and call "time" and give another short history lesson of Stockton, show the next technique and reveal early times of Stockton. As the day continues, the door to the gym will open and in walks Guro Dan's two remaining aunties. The first on is Auntie Arca wife of the late Albert Arca in which is Guro Dan's mother Mary Arca Inosanto, also walking in is his first cousins Paul and Al and there children. Coming in also is Auntie Flora Arca Motto, this is the sister of Guro Dan's Mother and Auntie Flora was the very first Filipino ever to be hired by the Stockton Unified School District. The room stops and Guro Run's over to embarrass them with joy. This is truly a priceless moment in time. Camera's and flashes take over as group shots of Guro Dan and his last remaining Aunties and cousins are taken. By this time stories and memories by Guro Dan's aunties are now taking over of Guro Dan or "Boom Boom's" childhood and early adult years. After a few minutes Guro Dan rushes back to the head of the class and calls "time", Guro Dan gives another short history

GRANDMASTER SOMERA'S WRITINGS

lesson of his childhood and relates all of this to Filipino Martial Arts and honoring his teachers. The next technique is now being given and is being shown to room full of students that is reflected in the technique that has not been shown in many years and is accelerated in the demonstration. As the first day comes to an end Master Adrian of Tandez Martial Art Academy from Mountain View, CA and Sifu Gonzalez of Western Martial Arts from Sacramento, CA along with his students are all amazed that have been treated to a very special session of Guro Dan's own childhood history and his history of growing up in Stockton. Everyone in the room has been treated to the first day as not only a day of outstanding training by Guro Dan but also a day of history of Filipino culture but also the personal life of Guro Dan.

As the second day begins the word must have spread throughout the San Joaquin valley that Guro Dan is working his magic with many of his Filipino Martial Art teachers along with the history that only Guro Dan can teach it. The lines are deep at the front door with the anticipation of Guro Dan walking up to the entrance door with all the knowledge of Filipino Martial Arts but also the History of how it came to be, but even more exciting is the stories that Guro Dan will share of this early years in Stockton, CA and the many Masters of the Filipino Arts that his had discovered from this little town that is known as "Little Manila".

Once again the room is packed with many students eager to learn with the worlds greatest Filipino Martial Art historian and player. Grand Master Art Mirlfor as a young man trained with Guro Dan during his training with Great Grand Master Angle Cables in Stockton during the early years of research was present with his school Knights of Escrima. With all eyes and ears ready to absorb what Guro Dan gives right away Guro Dan picks up for yesterdays seminar. As the day begins with the room is full of eager students and in walks the Carrido family in which Guro Dan grow up with. As Guro Dan noticed the group of old friends that enter the room a smile of joy take over his face and with grazed eyes Guro Dan rushes over to the Carrido family and embarrasses them all with hugs of joy. The first is Pat Carrido the youngest sister that Guro Dan would say, "when we were kids playing and during the time we would pick football teams I would pick Pat first because she could catch and run faster than anyone", the next hug with to Gloria Carrido Nomuma the retired vice mayor of Stockton and the first Filipino every to hold this rank in city government. As Guro Dan go to the next person Coach Frank Carrido grabs Guro Dan to embarrass him and share the good old times. Coach Frank Carrido is one of the greatest football coaches in our area and now is one of the most sought after high school coaches in California.

What a great treat for everyone in attendance, once again Guro Dan rushes to the front of the room and calls "time". As if his old town mates inspired Guro he

TONY SOMERA: In His Own Words

would his rate of play and intensity would be push to every ones limits. Guro Dan would review the technique and would explain the reason why this technique was done and why it was done nearly 100 years ago. By this time Guro would not only give us one technique to review but several and at one time there was 8 techniques to review. As the day moves forward the door to the gym would open once again and in walk Mel Suguitan Jr. who's was the father of Manong Mel Sr., which was one of Guro Dan teachers. It was only after Manong Mel Sr's death that Mel jr would be told by Guro Dan was his Escrima teacher and Guro Dan's mother Mary Arca Inosanto would tell Mel jr of an encounter that Manong Mel Sr had in Alaska, fighting off over 5 men that attach him in which Manong Mel Sr came out safe and sound but Mary could not say the same for the men that attached him. Mel Jr. is also one of the most sought after choral teachers in the state of California he is also famous for being in the all Filipino signing group the "Old Pinoys". Mel Jr's wife Addie Suguitan was also present; Addie is also a who's who of Stockton by being one of the Charter members of the Little Manila Foundation and an honored City of Stockton employee. Mel and Addie's Suguitan daughters were also in attendance with Tamara a MMA fighter promoter and writer along with sister Adrianna an accomplished support of the Stockton Filipino Community. Along with the Suguitan Pat Muraoka a member of the Filipino American Historical Society would accompany family and Stockton Buddhist Church in which will host the largest Obon Festival south of Sacramento, California. Pat is also a supporter of the Filipino community and is involved with all that takes place with both historical societies. Pat's son Alan was also there with many accomplishments within the Stockton Asian communities and surrounding areas. After all the hugs and short stories of the early days of Stockton and Guro Dan growing up many photos would be snapped and once again Guro Dan would rush back to the front of the class and call "time". Guro would move on with the next technique with even more intensity. With a big smile on Guro Dan's face he would reminisce about all of his visitors and would introduce them with rounds of applauses. Amongst this day we are also honor to have visitors like Master Carlito Bundoc of Mata Sa Bagyo Filipino Martial Arts Academy and Grand Master Max Pallen of Pallens Martial Arts, both coming to pay there respect and also train with the living ledgen Guro Dan Inosanto. What a great day that ended much to fast with both days going by like it was in speed. To communicate this great weekend Guro Dan shared with us many of his childhood stories of growing up in Stockton California and long with speaking of the great Bruce Lee and many of his Filipino Martial Art teachers. As many of know Guro Dan is like a walking goggle application that has endless information about martial arts in general but also the love and respect of

GRANDMASTER SOMERA'S WRITINGS

this teachers in which he gives all the recognition as he speaks about each technique that is given throughout both days. Training with Guro Dan is an honor and privilege that all of us had experienced and if you ever have the opportunity to train with this living legend Guro Dan Inosanto this writer highly recommends this to any type of practitioner of the Martial Arts for Guro Dan is gift from God that has blessed us in a way that no other martial artist can describe or has given information so freely to all of us. The best time to visit Guro Dan is when he is in his hometown of Stockton, California so that you can experience the things that all of has during his last visit here in the city nicknamed "Little Manila".

TONY SOMERA: In His Own Words

BANDA-BANDA:
THE STAFF OF GIRON ESCRIMA

The Giron system of arnis/escrima has a staff system called *banda-banda*, meaning side-side. In the Filipino martial arts, the staff is thought by many to be "secret," as it is rarely taught to anyone. This is evidenced by the fact that most articles on arnis show only techniques with the single stick.

The Filipino staff generally is a length of rattan measuring six feet, with a diameter of one-to-two inches. In simple terms, banda-banda is a long-range weapon art that uses a two-handed grip to maximize striking power and force on impact. The Giron banda-banda staff system has approximately 70 basic moments, encompassing the elements of blocking, deflection, evasion, and direct striking.

The staff is used to put an opponent out of commission quickly. To use this weapon effectively, the practitioner must be strong and well-versed in the estilo redonda, or circular style of offense and defense. Since the staff is long, it is used most effectively in the street or the cleared area of a parking lot.

The Giron banda-banda system uses two staff grips. The first features two hands held at one end of the weapon. If you are right-handed, the right hand will be positioned above the left hand, and vice-versa. With this type of grip, the basic cinco tero pattern is used, along with the redonda style of striking. The blocking grip is used in much the same fashion. The theory behind this grip is that you must keep your opponent at bay, and only when the opponent closes the distance does the second grip comes into play. In this grip, your hands are held a shoulder's width apart, dividing the staff into thirds. Both of these grips are used for blocking, deflecting, redirecting, and direct striking to the opponent's body or weapon.

The striking patterns used with the staff vary, depending on the situation. Normally, strikes come from the traditional arnis striking patterns, known as cinco tero (five strikes) and redonda (circular strikes). In order to acquire the proper striking habit, each motion must be followed through to its completion. In other words, don't stop the strike on impact but aim past the target. Moreover, foot and body movements must work together to create the maximum amount of torque in each technique. Once these two

GRANDMASTER SOMERA'S WRITINGS

striking sequences have been mastered, unorthodox movements can be developed based on the process of interpolation.

The novice also must learn how to relax and feel confident that the opponent's weapon may not necessarily inflict injury on him, and that such a painful experience can be avoided. Tenseness will result in slow reaction, impairing both timing and coordination. Until one becomes fairly skilled with the staff, one should not sacrifice safety by chancing an aggressive movement.

TONY SOMERA: In His Own Words

LARGA MANO: THE WARRIOR STYLE

Larga Mano, is one of the twenty styles of the Giron System of Arnis Escrima. Grand Master Emeritus Leo Giron defined Larga Mano by saying, "The term Larga Mano literally means "long hand," and implies the ability to extend one's reach. Reaching your opponent without jeopardizing safety is foremost because one can disable his enemy with less chance of getting hurt or killed. To employ this style, a practitioner must know how to use a longer weapon systematically. A person cannot just swing his longer weapon like a flail. It is an art and therefore must abide with the larga mano science. The practice of stretching far is the daily exercise of a larga mano practitioner. You need to understand the components of larga mano in order to maintain the control and accuracy of this combat."

Basic Fundamentals of Larga Mano

Body mechanics is an essential component of Larga Mano. When choosing the style of Larga Mano, the student must use proper body mechanics to use a weapon of such great length. Not only is a larga mano weapon extra long, but it also carries a significant increase in weight. Your entire body needs to work together in order to defend yourself. The feet need to be planted in a strong position in order to give you a solid foundation to strike. The legs need to balance and support the weight and force of your motion as you advance or retreat. Conditioning of your legs is mandatory in order to maintain your balance. Using your legs to stretch forward and back works in conjunction with operation of such a long weapon. Timing your legs with your hips also is necessary, much like a baseball pitcher when rotating his hips to deliver a pitch. The larga mano student must incorporate the rotation of his hips to deliver his ending strike to his opponent and his legs to retract the motion of his weapon in order to prepare himself for the next movement and oncoming enemies.

To simplify striking patterns, the larga mano system is adapted to only five strikes or what is called cinco tero. The striking patterns called cinco tero are taken from the term cabaroan, which means "new way" or "new style." The ancient warriors discovered that when swinging a long weapon, the first angle of attack is to the left side of the opponent targeting the base

GRANDMASTER SOMERA'S WRITINGS

of the neck. Slicing down diagonally to the right side of the opponent's right leg, the return strike will target the opponent's right ankle and return to the original angle up to the opponents left side of the neck. The third strike will circle from the opponent's left side to the opponent's left ankle, striking up diagonally to the opponent's right side base of the neck. The fourth strike will return in a downward strike to the opponent's right side base of the neck, cutting back down to the chamber on the right side of your hip ready to deliver the fifth and final blow. The fifth strike is a thrust to the opponent's midsection, targeting the bellybutton. With the length and weight of the larga mano weapon, it can be used to cover all striking angles just by using cinco tero, and all that is needed is to lower your body to cover the mid and lower angles of attack.

Terrain is another essential component of Larga Mano. Naturally, the perfect terrain or area to use larga mano is in an area that is open and free from any obstacles that might interfere with the cinco tero kabaroan strikes. Also, the ground should be flat and free from any obstacles. But this is not always the case, as during World War II when then Sergeant Leo M. Giron would need to adapt to the different terrain when defending himself in the jungles of the Philippines. Giron would plant himself using the de fondo style of Giron Arnis Escrima and use the components necessary to gain the

TONY SOMERA: In His Own Words

advantage to win in combat. Moving or jumping around could be very dangerous to you during an encounter. You may run the risk of twisting your ankle and falling down, cutting your own leg or falling down by losing your own balance. Grand Master Giron often would relate to us that terrain also may be your enemy if not used and thought of properly, but it can be your advantage if you know how to use it.

Distance is a major component of larga mano. Utilizing the length of your weapon is a must for any larga mano player. Keep in mind that even when using a shorter weapon, the concept of larga mano still is applied. Your body mechanics will apply, along with your striking pattern and the use of terrain fighting. But most importantly, your basic fundamentals will carry you through. You may have a shorter weapon but play larga mano by using all the basic fundamentals of a long weapon where applicable. Remember the true meaning of larga mano is using a longer weapon. While playing larga mano, keeping your distance is keeping you safe.

Finally, we must consider the fundamental of Timing. Timing your movement and strike to evade the attack of your opponent will allow for direct cuts into vulnerable targets of opportunity within the conflict.

In the middle of World War II, one year before any American soldiers landed on Philippine soil, then Technical Sergeant Leo M. Giron was

GRANDMASTER SOMERA'S WRITINGS

dropped off by submarine with a secret mission directly from General Douglas MacArthur to be his eyes and ears on the Philippine island of Luzon. Giron's mission was to send back vital information in preparation for the American invasion forces. Part of Sergeant Giron's mission was not to be detected. If he was detected, he was to eliminate any evidence of U,S, soldiers currently on Philippine soil. Armed with an M-1, a .45 colt, a 24-inch bolo knife, and a 36-inch talanason Giron and a small group of Filipino American commandos, along with a handful of native Filipino guerrillas, started their mission deep behind enemy lines.

During Giron's many encounters with the enemy, he had to use silent, deadly force. If Giron and his unit used their firearms, they would bring attention to their position and also risk alerting the enemy that U.S. soldiers had landed with the intention of retaking the Philippine Islands and liberating the native Filipinos from their cruel captors.

Giron would depend on his 24-inch bolo knife and 36-inch talanason. The bolo knife was used mainly to clear brush, creating a narrow path through the thick jungle for his patrol. On rare occasions during close quarter encounters, Giron would use his 24-inch bolo knife to protect himself and his unit from the enemy. But, in nearly all of Giron's encounters with the enemy, he would use his 36-inch talanason to counter the long bayonets and samurai swords that were being swung at Giron's head to chop him down. Giron would counter his enemy with his talanason, using Larga Mano. By combining combatively body mechanics, cinco tero striking patterns, terrain management, larga mano distancing and timing, GME Giron was able to keep himself safe in the Philippine jungles and complete his mission.

Applying your basic fundamentals is the secret to defending any form of attack and can be used no matter what style of martial arts you are playing. Larga Mano encompasses many different components. In order for the student to play larga mano, students need to understand that the weapon of choice is one that will range in length from 30 to 36 inches. This understanding must include the knowledge of what it may take to handle a weapon of this great length. Just like any martial art that has its own style, you will need to understand the basic fundamentals in order to master the style.

GIRON ESCRIMA TECHNIQUES

TONY SOMERA: In His Own Words

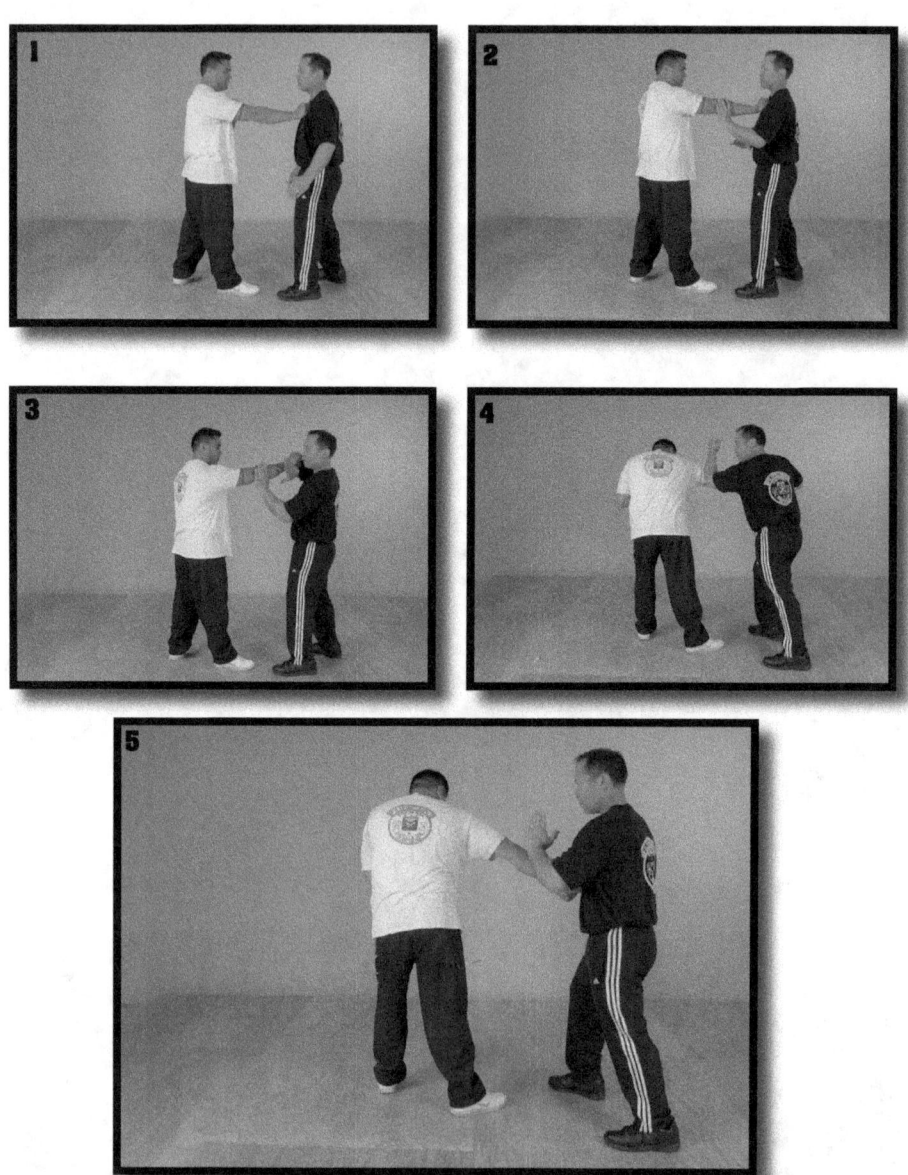

SINGLE LAPEL GRAB 1. Master Joel Juanitas grabs Guro Somera lapel with his right hand. 2. Grandmaster Somera controls the opponent's right elbow with his left hand... 3. ...and passes his right hand under to... 4. ...grab his right wrist and apply pressure... 5. in order to start an elbow pushing down lock.

GIRON ESCRIMA TECHNIQUES

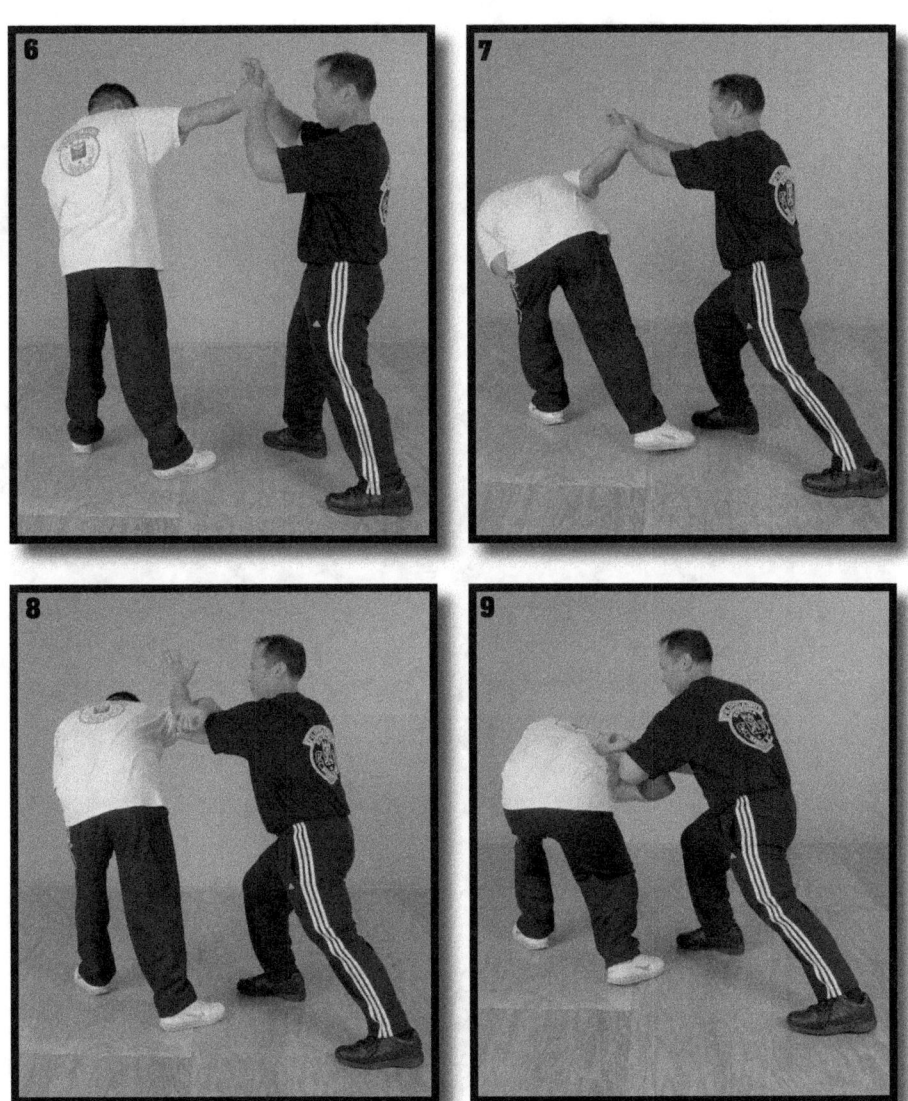

6. From there Guro Somera grabs the wrist and... 7. ...applies downward pressure in wristlock ... 8... as a variation, inserts his left arm... 9. ...and finished with an bent-elbow lock.

TONY SOMERA: In His Own Words

SINGLE LAPEL GRAB OPPOSITE VIEW NOTE: This sequence shows the previous techniques but from a frontal angle when the details of the elbow attack, the wrist control y the final bent-arm lock are more clearly visible.

GIRON ESCRIMA TECHNIQUES

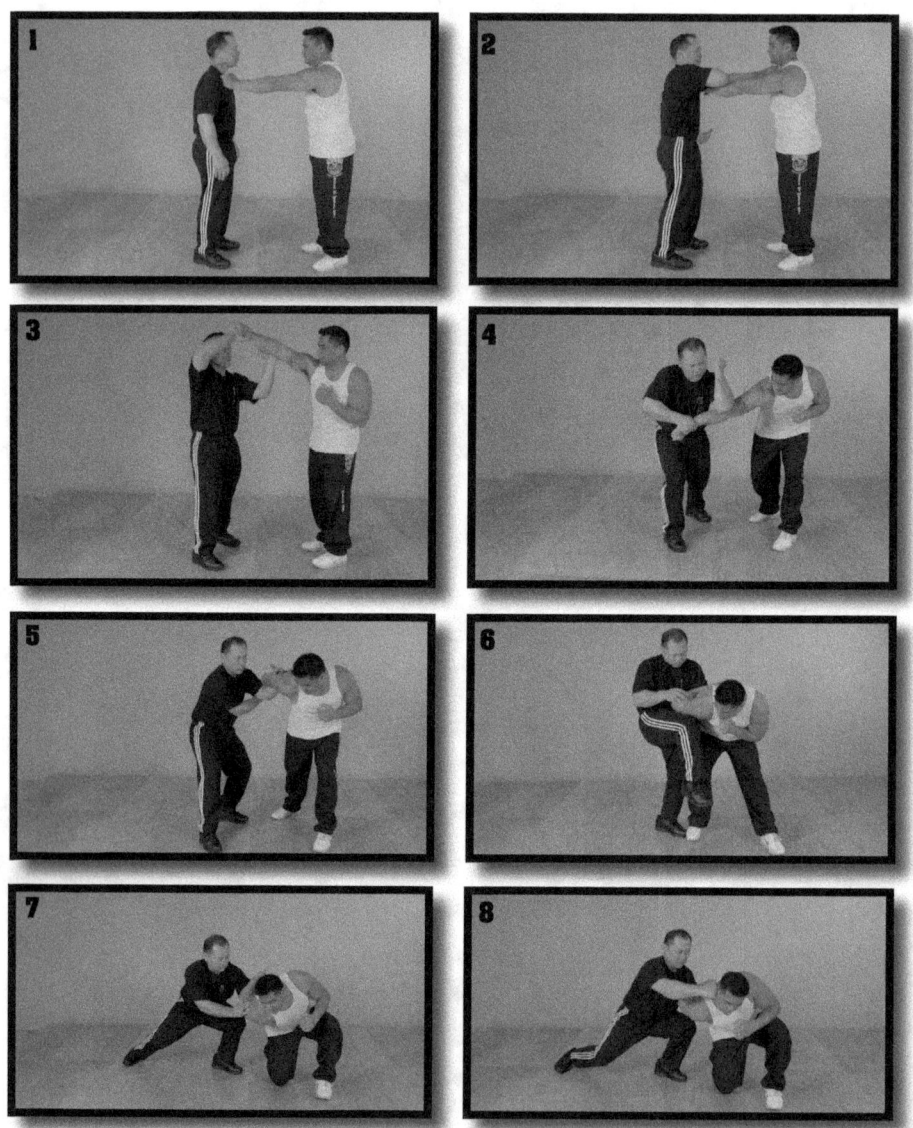

DOUBLE LAPEL GRAB 1. Aggressor grabs Guro Somera with both hands. 2. Guro Somera uses his right hand to grab the opponent's left wrist. 3. With the assistance of his left hand controlling the opponents right elbow... 4. ...applies downward pressure to start... 5. ...a bent-arm lock... 6. ...followed by an upward knee to the shoulder. 7. By retreating his right foot, brings his opponent to the ground... 8. ...to finish him off with a punch to the face.

GIRON ESCRIMA TECHNIQUES

DOUBLE NECK GRAB 1. Opponent grabs Grandmaster Somera neck with both hands. 2. Guro Somera immediately strikes with his right hand palm the opponent's chin. 3. Using his right hand, brings the aggressor's left arm down... 4. ...and pushes up the right elbow to open the angle for... 5. ...and reverse bent-arm lock. 6. The aggressor attempts to strike with his left hand but Guro Somera uses his right hand to deflect the attack... 7. ...an applies a double arm lock. 8. Then, he finishes him off with a punch to the face.

TONY SOMERA: In His Own Words

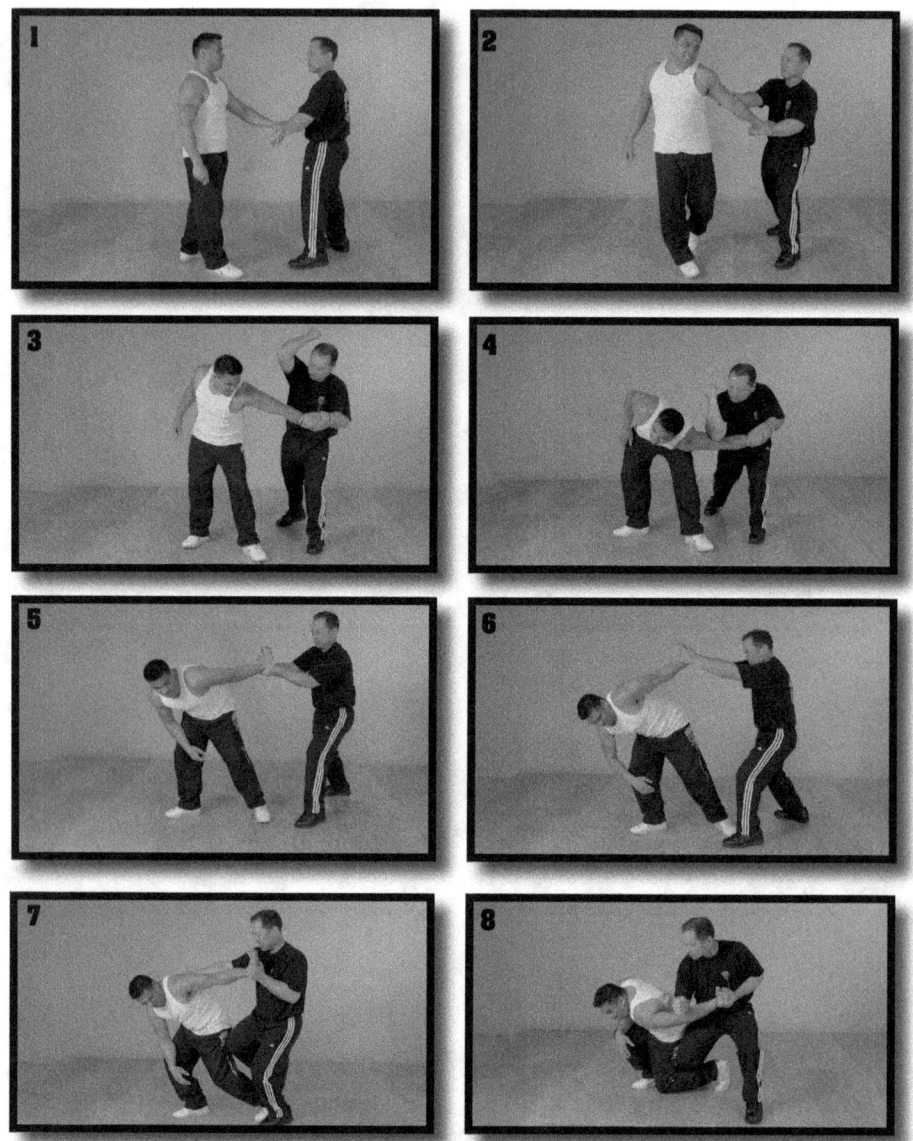

REVERSE WRIST GRAB 1. The aggressor grabs Guro Somera left wrist. 2. Guro Somera steps to the side and apply pressure on the opponent's left elbow... 3. ...following up with.... 4. ...downward elbow strike to break the opponent's arm. 5. Immediately, brings his right hands to grab the aggressor's hand with two hands and... 6. ...creates space to... 7. ...apply a knee strike to the side of the opponent's tight... 8. ...in order to fully control him on the ground.

GIRON ESCRIMA TECHNIQUES

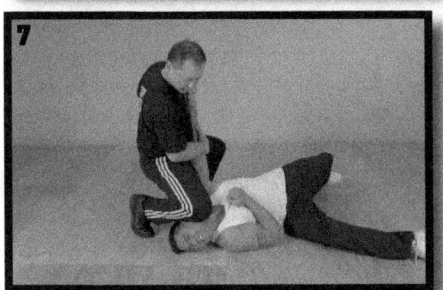

WRIST GRAB FROM THE BACK
1. Aggressor grabs Grandmaster Somera' right wrist from behind. 2. Guro Somera turns and... 3. ...in a counterclockwise movement of his left hand... 4. ...reverses the grip to bring the opponent down. 5. But when he feels the opponent's retraction of his left hand... 6. ...Guro Somera moves his right foot in a clockwise direction to take the aggressor down... 7. ...and control him on the floor with the right knee pinning the head.

TONY SOMERA: In His Own Words

BEAR HUG FROM THE BACK 1. Master Kirk McCune grabs Guro Somera from behind. 2. With his left hand, Grandmaster Somera releases the grip while turning his body and... 3. ...applies and upward elbow attack. 4. Followed by a movement of his right foot in a clockwise direction... 5. ...that allows him to apply a bent-arm lock... 6. ...and a final upward knee strike to the opponent's shoulder joint.

GIRON ESCRIMA TECHNIQUES

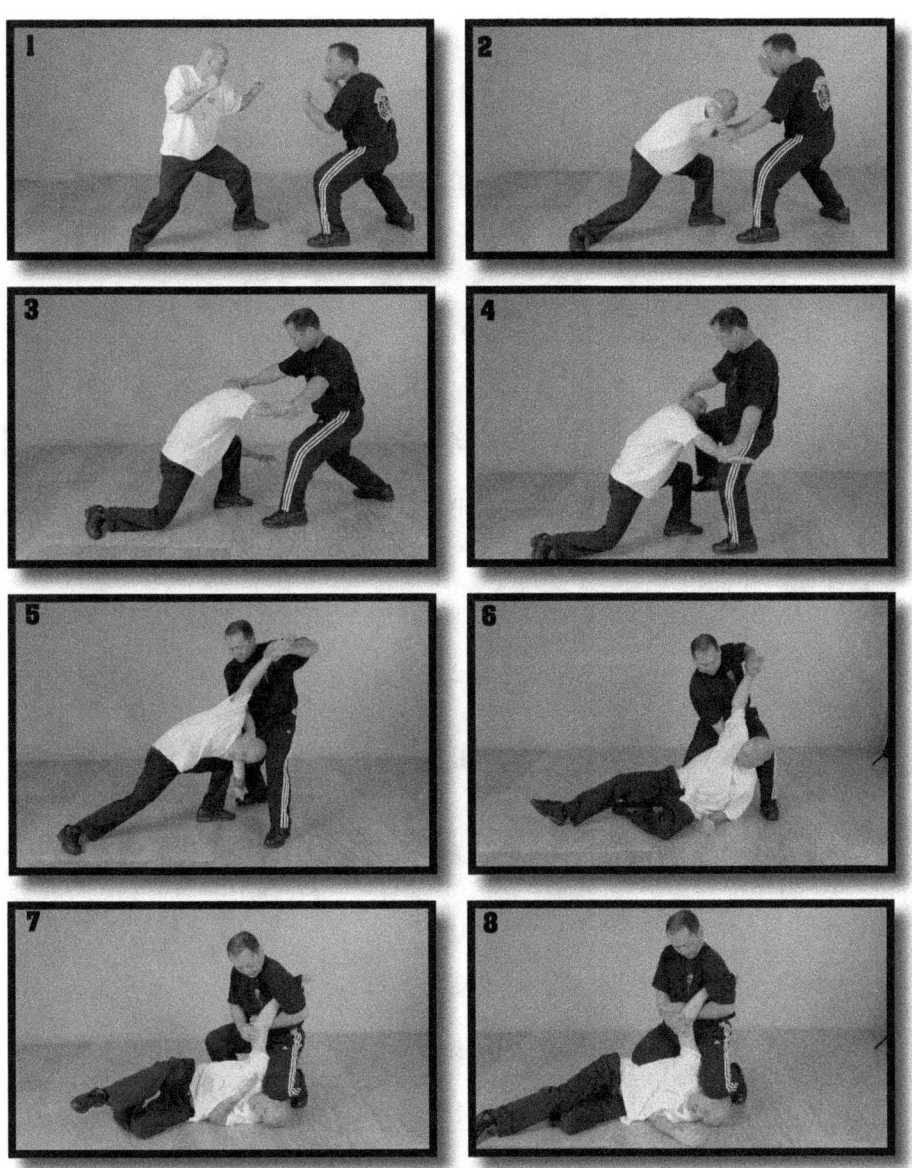

DEFENSE AGAINST TACKLE 1. Grandmaster Somera facing his opponent. 2. The aggressor begins to close the distance to tackle him... 3. ...but Guro Somera steps back with his right foot to create space, control the head and... 4. ...applies an upward knee strike. 5. With the right hand, turns the opponent's head around... 6. ...and brings him to the ground... 7. ..where he can control the arm... 8. ...to apply a finishing hold controlling him with both knees.

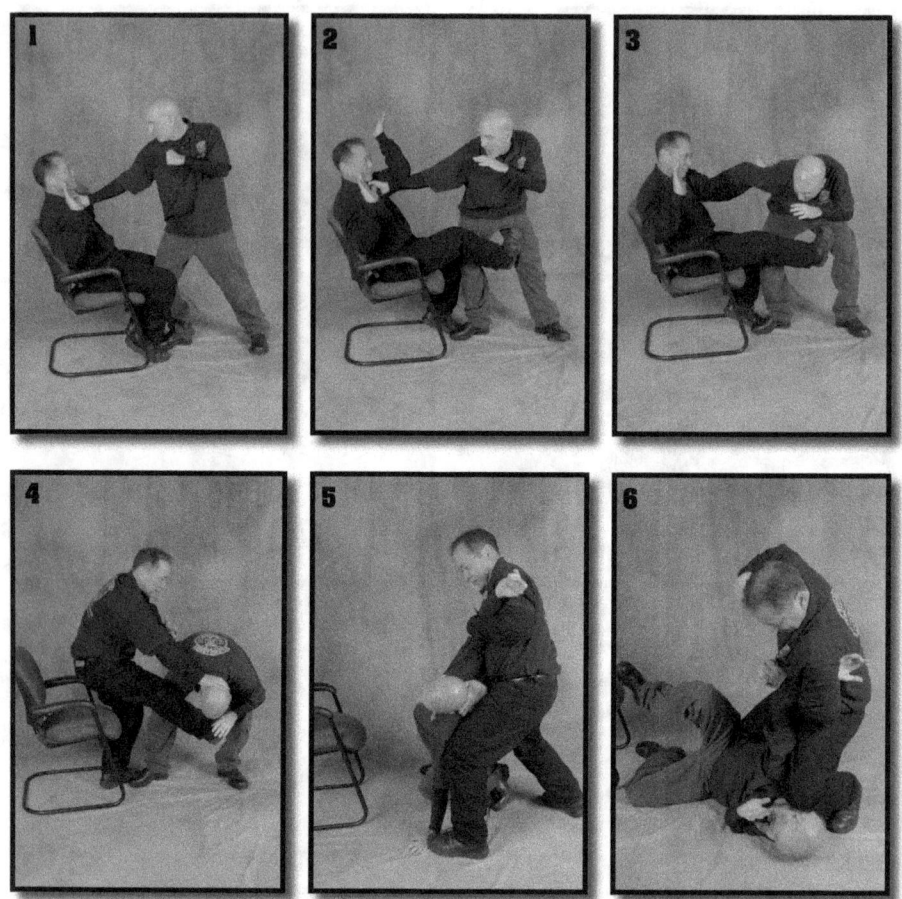

FRONTAL LAPEL GRAB ON A CHAIR 1. Aggressor grabs GM Somera lapel. 2. Guru Somera circles his left hand around the opponent's right arm... 3. ...as simultaneously delivers a kick to the inside of the left leg. 4. Then, he stands up and controlling the aggressor's head... 5. ...circles around to bring him onto the ground... 6. ...where he controls him and finishes him off.

GIRON ESCRIMA TECHNIQUES

SHOULDER GRAB FROM THE SIDE 1. Aggressor grabs GM Somera's left shoulder. 2. By using his left hand, Guru Somera pushed his opponent's right arm up... 3. ...and begins to apply an armlock as he stands up. 4. Then, he moves his right foot back and put pressure down on the armlock ... 5. ...to bring his opponent down... 6. ...and finish him off with a upward right knee strike to the head.

TONY SOMERA: In His Own Words

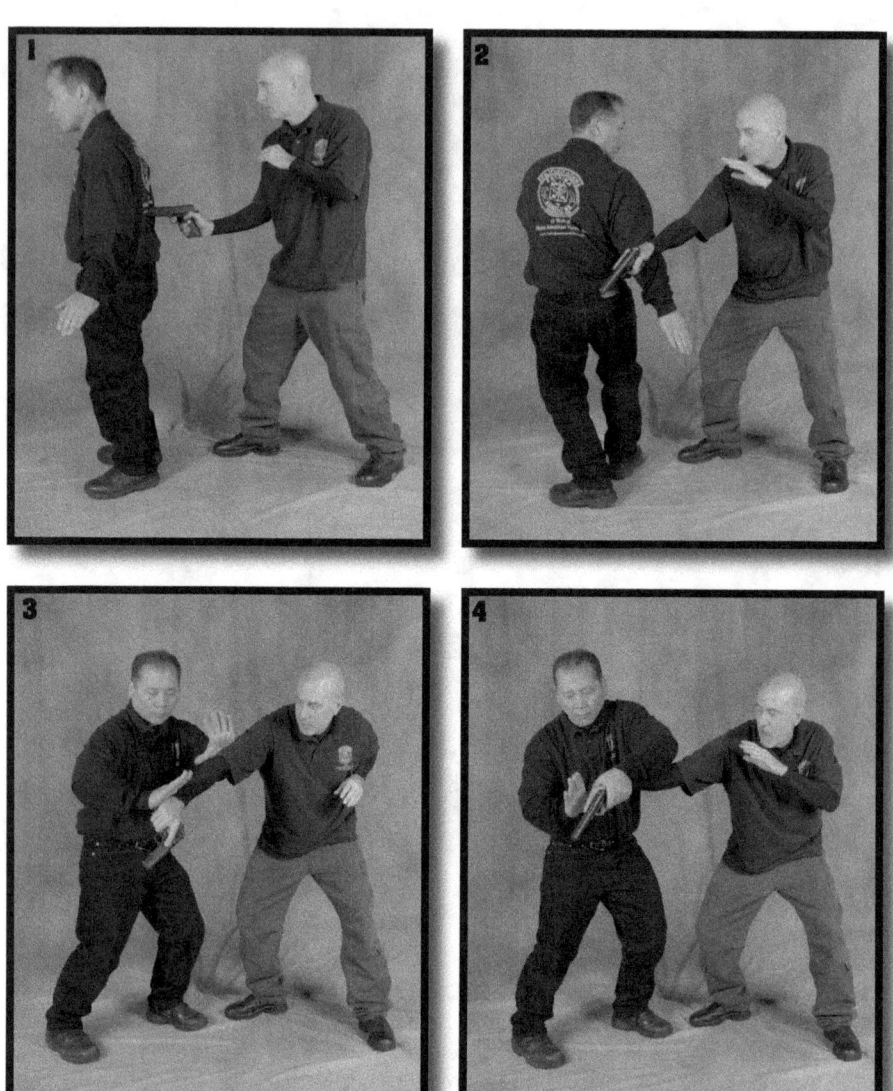

POINTING GUN FROM THE BACK 1. Aggressor hold a gun pointing to GM Somera's back. 2. GM Somera circles back around toward his right side and deflects the gun. 3. Immediately he uses his left hand to control the gun... 4. ...and slides his left hand toward to aggressor's right wrist.

GIRON ESCRIMA TECHNIQUES

5. Then, he applies a wristlock... 6. ... in order to disarm the aggressor. 7. GM Somera finalizes the defense taking the opponent's gun and pointing it at him.

KNIFE ATTACK FROM THE FRONT 1. The aggressor has a knife pointing to GM Somera's throat. 2. Guru Somera moves his right foot in a circular pattern and deflects the weapon with his left hand. 3. Then, he uses his right hand to control the aggressor's right wrist... 4. ...and by stepping forward with his left foot, applies pressure to...

GIRON ESCRIMA TECHNIQUES

5. ...deliver a straight armbar control... 6. ...that allows him to proceed to insert his left hand under the opponent's arm... 7. ...to create a bent-arm lock that ends up pointing the aggressor's weapon into his own throat.

TONY SOMERA: In His Own Words

BLADE DEFENSE AGAINST ANGLE #2 1. GM Somera faces his opponent. 2. The opponent delivers and angle #2 attack to what Guro Somera responds directly blocking the attacking arm before the blade reaches its destination. 3. By controlling the opponent's right arm to prevent any further action... 4. ... GM Somera delivers a straight thrust to the opponents body.

GIRON ESCRIMA TECHNIQUES

STICK DEFENSE AGAINST ANGLE #2 1. Guro Somera is facing his opponent. 2. When the attacker delivers an angle #2 attack, Guro Somera uses a "shield" block to deflect the attack but supplementing the deflection with a control of his left "alive" hand. 3. Then, he follows up with a downward strike to the wrist... 4. ...and a final "push away" the attacking limb of the aggressor.

TONY SOMERA: In His Own Words

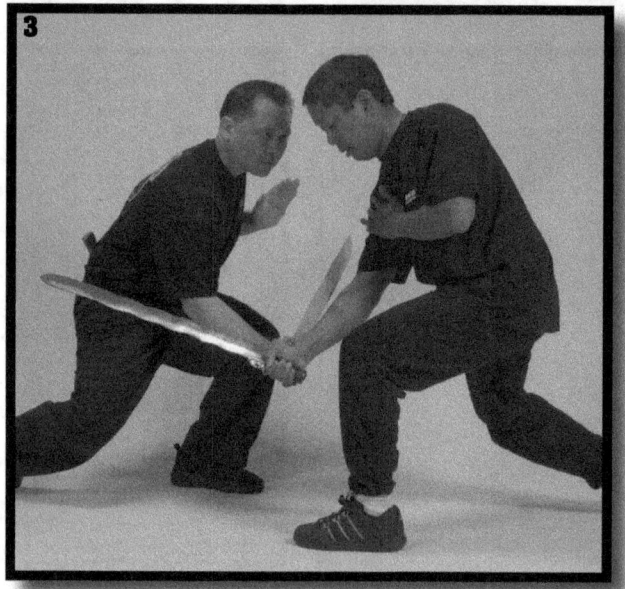

DEFENSE AGAINST THRUST ON ANGLE #5 1. GM Somera faces his opponent... 2. ...who attacks with a straight thrust to the midsection. GM Somera anticipates the attack and intercept the attack with his left hand, even before the attack gets his final delivery. 3. Then, he finishes the opponent's off with a downward cut to the forearm.

FACE OFF WITH
GM TONY SOMERA

What you consider your greatest achievement?

Embrace life for all it has given me.

What is your idea of perfect happiness?

Health.

Which talent would you most like to have?

Understanding.

What do you dislike most?

Being treated unfairly.

Which historical figure do you most identify with?

My father and his generation.

What is your favorite occupation?

Teacher.

What trait do you most deplore in others?

Violence.

What is your favorite journey?

Returning home.

What do you consider the most overrated virtue?

Beauty.

What is your greatest regret?

Not having enough time to help.

What or who is greatest love of your life?

Sally, my wife, and my family.

What quality do you like most in a man?

Honesty.

What is your favorite book?

The Bible.

What is the thing you would never do?

Betrayal.

How would you like to die?

In peace with God.

GIRON ESCRIMA MEMORIES OF A BLADED WARRIOR

By Grandmaster Leo M. Giron

Due largely to its effectiveness, Escrima is one of the world's most popular martial arts systems. Grandmaster Leo M. Giron designed this method to overcome a larger and stronger opponent in life-or-death encounters. Giron's Escrima contains many ingenious exercises and strategies while remaining the essence of simplicity. Giron's Escrima knowledge has been in great demand by thousands of Escrima, Arnis, and Kali students from all over the world—
and now for the first time, the original work of Grandmaster Giron is brought to the public with the most comprehensive information ever published in an Escrima book. Packed with photos taken with painstaking care to assure correct positioning and execution, this volume covers all of the fundamental and advanced principles as taught by the late Grandmaster Leo M. Giron.

US $45.00
www.martialartsdigital.com

ESCRIMA MASTERS
By Jose M. Fraguas

A rare and definitive book featuring the top masters of the Filipino Martial Arts of Escrima, Kali and Arnis. This outstanding compilation gathers the best masters in one comprehensive volume. In their own words, they explain the philosophy, training and spirit of the art. This book gives rare insights into the physical, mental, and spiritual methods that have enabled these chosen few to reach the pinnacles of the Filipino Martial Arts. Dan Inosanto, Ben Largusa, Leo Giron, Edgar Sulite, Cacoy Canete, Rene Latosa
– just to name a few – share thoughts and experiences in rare interviews that define the essence of their martial arts mastery.
For the first time, interviews with some of the world's top Escrima/Kali/Arnis masters have been gathered together in one book. No matter how well you think you know these masters, you haven't truly experienced their wit, wisdom, and insight until you have read "Escrima Masters"!

US$39.95
www.martialartsdigital.com

NOTES

NOTES

NOTES